GW00469525

# Instascam: Inside The Murky World Of Instagram Scammers

James Billington

**ACKNOWLEDGMENTS**

Thanks to my wife Sam who incredibly still says she loves me after all these years of acting like a wally.  Thanks also to Rob, Martin, Delayna, Pad, Nick, Ce, Vicky and Stew for their advice, advice, advice, advice, advice, advice, advice and advice respectively.

## INTRODUCTION

Hello. I'm James. I hope you're well. Quite rainy today, isn't it? You're looking good. Have you lost weight? I like your jumper. Thanks for purchasing this book. Sorry, no refunds.

Now that we've got the awkward introductions out of the way, let me tell you a little bit about what you're about to read. This book that you currently hold looks at the murky world of scammers across Instagram and other outlets of social media. We're going to take a deep dive into some of the seriously silly scenarios I've got myself involved in over the last three years whilst conversing with (mostly) Nigerian scammers.

You'll read tales involving love declarations, wedding proposals, a kidnapped mum, a sexy threesome involving a dog, a £2 million armed robbery theatre play, the purchase of a thousand ducks, an awkward conversation with two Keanu Reeves's and much more. What is the plural of Keanu Reeves? Keanu Reeveses? Keanu Reevi? Also, what's the name for a collective of Keanu Reeves? A Matrix? Maybe my next book could be about finding out what the plural of Keanu Reeves is and where that takes me? It would certainly be an Excellent Adventure...

Whilst the book has some MegaLolz™, I'll show you the other side of Instagram scams. We'll be looking at the people behind the fake accounts. You'll read interviews from scammers living in Nigeria talking about what they do, and why they look to defraud people online.

We'll also be looking at Instagram as a company too – and what they are doing to help combat scams and fraud across their platform.

It's taken me over three years to put this book together. For me, it's been an insightful journey looking at scammers and what they will do to try to extort money from people. I've learned all the different scams that people use on Instagram, and I'll share them with you too – to keep you clued up and on the lookout to make sure you don't get caught out. You'll also learn how to keep your account safe too.

So, together, we are going to go on a little journey. You'll get to meet all my new Instagram friends. Step onboard the HMS Scam Ship as I navigate you through the murky waters of con men, cheats, hackers and swindlers.

## BACK TO THE BEGINNING

Let's start this book off by saying: scammers are dishonest people. This book may be a light-hearted look at one man replying to scammers on Instagram. However, for scammers and hackers - it's big business. According to the annual fraud report by UK Finance, £1.2 billion was stolen by criminals through authorised and unauthorised fraud in 2022, the equivalent to £2,300 every minute.

That figure will actually be dramatically higher as many people who've been scammed won't have told the relevant authorities.

For the most part, it can be quite easy to spot a scam. It could be an email arriving in your junk folder stating you've been left $25,000,000 by a Nigerian prince; but as silly and ridiculous as these can be – scammers are always looking for ways to try to get you to part with your cash.

For you, it can be a silly email that you instantly delete and block. For vulnerable people however, it can be life changing. For me, a man with too much time on his hands, it's an opportunity to waste scammers time, phone data and try to get their account shut down. This means 93-year-old Doris, who doesn't know any better, is not losing her pension and life savings to these crooks. OMG, unless Doris is in on it too[1].

Scammers will use a variety of ways to try to get your money, and they're getting better at it. Although it's sometimes quite funny to look at the strange and silly ways these scammers will go to getting your money, do remember there is a serious side.

So... back to the beginning.

In 2021, when we all thought that the pandemic was over and LadBaby was only on his third Christmas number one (halcyon days I'm sure we can all agree), I started a new Instagram account. It started as a very silly unofficial fan account for someone I know. I won't post the profile here to keep them anonymous.

However, I would post pictures once a week or so with such 'hilarious' captions such as *'This is me, pictured in 2018 whilst thinking about hash browns'* or *'Just caught myself thinking about a time when I didn't know what marbles were'* and *'Just finished the final episode of Soldier Soldier. I'd recommend watching Soldier Soldier, especially if you have never watched an episode of Soldier*

---

[1] Huge if true.

*Soldier'*. As you'd expect, this sort of content blew up the internet. Some of the likes on the posts went into the double figures. Well, I think one did. And I may have accidentally liked that photo myself.

After a while however, things changed with that account. The account started gaining more and more followers. I was only posting sporadically, but the account was growing by around 40-50 followers a day. Who was I, KSI? I looked in the mirror to see if I was KSI. I asked people on the street 'Am I KSI?' Most people said no. Some people even walked to the next bus stop to avoid answering the question. I texted friends. I spoke to my family. 'Dad, am I KSI'? I looked in the mirror again. I had to accept it. I am not and never have been KSI – the YouTuber and co-founder of the Prime energy drink. Fun fact: Did you know Prime is only sold in boxes of 2, 3, 5, 7, 11, 13, 17, 19, 23, 29 etc[2]?.

As a result of gaining all my new followers, I changed the name of the account and called the person 'Pippa Pegg'. It also seemed that my new followers didn't recognise what sex I was either, so they would message calling me 'sexy' if they thought I was a woman or 'handsome' if they thought I was a guy. It was 2021. It was an odd time.

So, why was the account gaining so many followers? I delved deeper. On closer inspection, I noticed that the majority of my new followers were from new Instagram accounts. Their profile pictures were also striking, often of a sexy man or attractive woman, or they were from an account promoting a get rich quick scheme. As they were new accounts, most of the profiles had very few photos posted too. Some hadn't posted any photos at all. However, every time a new account started following me, they would always send me a direct message.

Always.

Every half an hour or so, my phone would ping to tell me someone had slid into my DM's (do the kids still say this?) Messages like this would appear in my inbox.

*'Hi'*
*'Hello'*
*'How are you doing?'*
*'Hello. I hope you and your family are well.'*

As a man with a penchant for mischief, I'd reply to their DM messages[3]. I'd

---

[2] Strap yourself in if that sort of joke is up your street.
[3] Can you say 'DM messages' when in reality it translates as 'Direct Message Messages',

always reply and be super friendly. The more I did this, the more and more of these accounts would come out of the woodwork. Within a couple of months, I had over 4,000 followers. I felt like I was Kerry Katona, circa 2004. Every single one of the 4,000 accounts that followed me were fake accounts.

Every. Single. One.

It seemed that interacting with a scammer by liking a photo on their newsfeed or commenting on a picture was like awakening a hornet's nest. I was swamped with scammers following me, liking and commenting on my photos and always, always sending me a DM.

They were all fake accounts run by scammers – meaning the accounts were real, but the profile picture didn't match the person operating the account[4]. I knew the messages coming through to me were scammers because in general, the conversations were all very similar. The dialogue all followed a certain formula, and their English, although good, was never quite perfect[5].

Scammers will scour the internet for pictures of people to create their perfect profile. If it's a man, it will usually be a ruddy great hunk with those things that sit on top of their arms[6], smiling and having eyes that you could drown in. If the account was a woman, she was usually in very little clothing and had breasts that made her look like she was photobombing a Right Said Fred selfie. Scammers create their profile by using real people's pictures from the internet and taking on that person's identity.

A recent article in MailOnline stated that fitness model Farren Morgan, who at the time had over 220,000 Instagram followers, had his pictures used by scammers. He has been the face of countless Instagram and TikTok scams, as criminals used his photos to take advantage of vulnerable women. Farren was quoted as saying 'At one point Instagram actually deleted my own account and said I was the fake one while the other accounts were still scamming people. I was really stressed out because my business was doing really well at the time, and I couldn't get hold of anyone at Instagram'.

My first piece of advice is to be careful if you're really good looking and are often using hashtags such as #ShreddedLife, #FlexFriday, #DoYouEvenLift, #SheSquatsBro and #SunsOutGunsOut[7].

---

in the say way we say 'PIN number'.
[4] Yeah, a bit like my account I suppose. Et tu reader.
[5] Yeah, a bit like this book I suppose. Et tu reader.
[6] Muscles.
[7] Could also be the marketing tagline for Florida's tourism board.

As stated, there would always be a formula for these conversations. It would always start with a direct message and then would quickly move on to ask the following questions:

**Where are you from?**
The reason a scammer asks this question is they want to make sure you live in a prosperous and rich country. According to Analytics Insight, most scammers on Instagram will be Nigerian males, normally aged between 16-20, and they want to make sure they are speaking to someone from the west – as they believe that everyone in the west is rich. If you're living in the USA or UK – perfect!

**What do you do for a living?**

They want to know you have a regular income coming in – and that you have money! It doesn't matter what your job is (we'll come on to that later), they just want to know you have a steady income. They may also ask if you own your own house and car.

**What is your relationship status?**

Many of the scams involve trying to get you to fall in love with them. Scammers will give you an array of compliments to make you feel special. They'll ask you to send a picture, and when you do, they'll shower you with compliments. *'OMG you beautiful* bbe' *'Wow, you stunning' 'GTFOH hun, you is the gritz*[8]*'* etc, but they need to know you are single for this to happen. They'll also ask if you have 'kids'. The word they use is always 'kids', never 'children'.

**How is your family?**

Scammers are looking to get an emotional hold over you. They want to contact people who are lonely or vulnerable. Ideally, they don't want you to have a family, or contact with family or friends – because they don't want you to speak to them about your 'new wonderful relationship' on Instagram. The more people that know what's going on – the more chance the scammer will be discovered. It's a bit sad really, but they are looking to target lonely and vulnerable people.

You might think that this is all quite unbelievable – but I have had countless communications from scammers saying they are in love with me after five messages or just 10 minutes of conversation. They'll do anything to try to build a relationship – and for you to get you to trust them. Once they have gained your trust, they can attempt to exploit you for whatever it is they want. In the

---

[8] Really trying to get this expression to take off.

real world it takes months and months to build up a relationship like this – but in the filter-heavy shadowy world of Instagram, time is money, so scammers need to work quickly.

So, how can you spot a scam account on Instagram? Scammer accounts will usually have less followers than people they follow. They'll follow lots of people and message as many people as possible. The more people they contact, the more chance of someone messaging back. As soon as they do, they've got an opening. It's the classic *'throw enough shit at a wall and see what sticks'* approach. An approach I used when talking to women in nightclubs circa 1999-2001[9].

Another trait about these accounts is that most scammers will only have posted a few photos – which is always a red flag. Unless they've posted pictures of an actual red flag. That's just a red flag and that's broadly fine. Some scammers will also buy fake Instagram followers to increase their follower count to make their account look more legitimate. Most of the accounts will be new, a few weeks old, but they might have posted many photos in a short space of time to give the impression the account looks legitimate.

Once a conversation starts flowing, and you have answered the relevant questions, they will do whatever they can to get money off you. They will lie, manipulate and do whatever they can to get you to part with your honk[10]. Before that happens though, once a conversation has started, a scammer will ask if they can continue the conversation away from Instagram and move to a different platform, such as Google Chat or Telegram. It's important that a scammer does this.

They want the conversation to move away from Instagram for one simple reason – they want to protect their Instagram account. Their account is important to them and it's their way in to access more victims.

As a result, a scammer may tell you that they are not on Instagram much, or as part of their job, they are not allowed to be on Instagram, so they need to move the conversation to another platform. They will be really insistent on this, and guilt trip you, telling you that to continue the conversation, you will need to speak to them on Google Chat or Telegram. Take note that it's not WhatsApp. Google Chat and Telegram is all done through email, whereas WhatsApp is done through your phone number. Therefore, once they give you their phone number for WhatsApp chatter, you will be able to tell from the

---

[9] Although, why I was taking excrement to nightclubs is anyone's guess.
[10] Money. Been trying to get that word to take off since 2005. No such luck.

international code that they are not from where they say they are.

This meant I had to download Google Chat and continue conversations with these scammers on both Instagram and Google Chat. At one point, my current wife (always keep her on her toes by using that term) asked why my phone had just received so many notifications flashing up. 'Chill out babe' I said, 'it's just Brad Pitt messaging me on Google Chat – talking to me about him being stuck on his latest movie set and asking me for help in buying him an iTunes voucher for his children'. At some point, some university student will do a thesis looking at how I'm still married.

At one point, I did think about getting a burner phone and using it solely for scammers, but I did realise that 'current' wife can very quickly turn into 'ex' wife and therefore thought better of it.

It's been reported by business publication The Information, that 10% of all Instagram accounts are fake – that's a whopping 95 million in total! This includes scam accounts, bots, fake celebrity accounts and Kanye West – who at this point might be an amalgamation of all of these. This means there are plenty of scammers out there all looking to extort money off you.

Hopefully that's a nice little introduction into the weird world of Instagram scammers. But I will tell you now, things will get a little weird.

Well, a lot weird.

I have put together some of my favourite conversations with scammers over the last couple of years and show you the conversations I have had with them. The book will break down the different types of tricks that these swindlers use on Instagram to get you to part with your money. Each chapter will focus on a particular scam, and you'll see some of the very ridiculous chats I've had with scammers. So, grab a cup of tea[11] and enjoy me wasting scammers time (and actually quite a lot of my own).

Despite the chapters silly exchanges, online scamming is a serious topic and can ruin lives. I didn't just want this book to be solely stories of the silly conversations I have got involved with. There's a look at the reasoning as to why scammers do what they do – and how having a mobile phone for them opens up a whole world on how they can extort money.

There's also Instagram themselves. As one of the biggest companies in the world, they must have some pretty strict practices in place to stop scams

---

[11] Or a large glass of wine for the chapter titled 'Add Ralph'.

happening on their platform. Right? We'll look into that too. I hope that the book gives you some insight into the murky world of Instagram.

You might think that 'The 'Gram' is all cat photos and pictures of people on holiday. Dig beneath the surface and it's a bit of a murky world. Don't worry though, we'll go through it together.

## HOOK-UP SCAM

The first scam we are going to look at is 'hook-up'. The hook-up scam is pretty simple really. Sexy ladies (well, scammers with sexy ladies as their profile picture) would start a conversation as a direct message. Their profile would have pictures of them looking coquettish, in little clothing. The kind of photo you might see in the middle section of the Littlewoods catalogue in 1991.

Their bio would read something along the lines of *'Looking for hook-up. Only real people. No scammers please'*. Oh, the irony. Once they have asked your name and age – the next important question is 'Where are you from?'. I would always reply saying I am from the England, and miraculously – out of the 195 countries in the world, they too would also live in England.

Their next question would also be 'Where abouts in England do you live?'. For this, I would reply back with numerous responses. London, Nottingham, Luton, Slough, Stafford[12]. Again, miraculously, they would say they were nearby. What are the chances? Once they say they are close by, they will then ask if you are interested in a hook up. I mean, who isn't interested in some sexy lady time with some sexy strangers who lives close by? The scammer continues to send through provocative pictures to you, to entice you that this is indeed a real situation.

Who doesn't want to have friends with benefits? When I was a younger man, I certainly had quite a few friends with benefits. Actually, looking back, it was friends *on* benefits[13].

However, the scam begins when the scammer will ask for $50 or so to 'get gas' to come over. They might also ask to get a steam/iTunes/gift card on the way over and they will repay you when they arrive. Obviously, this never occurs, and you lose the $50. It's a story as old as time. Here are some very silly examples of me wasting a scammers time with the hook-up con.

---

[12] Straight outta Stafford.
[13] New Labour, new danger!

**ECONOMIES OF SCALE**

### Victoria jason

victoria_jason1994 · Instagram

View profile

Let me introduce you to Victoria Jason. Despite the name and ambiguous profile picture, the scammer was pretending to be a man. And what a man he was. Victoria Jason (or should it be Jason Victoria) messaged me and in no uncertain terms wanted to have sex with me. Actual sex with actual me.

Victoria Jason (let's call him Jason from now on) was blunt and to the point. They said that we should meet up for some short bursts of love making. After a few short messages, he had this to say.

I can duck your pussy so bad

I charge for it baby I can come over and fuck you real bad

Did he mean 'fuck'? Did he mean 'duck'? Was it a simple spelling error? Could this autocorrect lead to a giant business deal? There was only one way to find out. I messaged back.

Can you get me a duck?

Please

I need a good duck

Jason wasn't prepared for this. He had to pivot. From offering his dangly parts, he decided to change course. He swapped anatomy for Anatidae. Yes, of course Jason had a duck to sell me.

> Depending on how many duck
> you want

> Per duck is $50

A pretty good deal I'm sure you'll agree. I needed a good ducking and I need a good ducking fast. Finally, a sentence where autocorrect says the right thing. My new Instagram friend Jason was a supplier of ducks, and I was the duck customer.

Jason asked me if I wanted the ducks dead or alive. Good question – I hadn't thought of that to be honest. I mean, it's not like I was making this up on the fly. I worked out my finances. Each duck was $50. How many ducks could I afford? How many ducks could Jason supply?

> Ok each duck is $50

> I need 1,000 ducks

Yeah, sounds about right. I was a man who needed 1,000 ducks. Has anyone ever asked for one thousand ducks? Was this a world first? What would I do with 1,000 ducks? So many questions from my end. Jason though, to his credit, kept their business head on and wanted to proceed with the transaction as quickly as possible.

> Okay I wil get them

> You have to send me $500 to
> get it now

$500? That's probably a duck deposit. That's how the business works I presume. I had to make sure that Jason knew I was a serious businessman, and I was very specific with Jason the types of ducks I desired. So, I sent Jason a very detailed list of the quantity and type of ducks I needed.

> This is what I need:
>
> 90 Aylesbury ducks
> 100 Bali ducks
> 100 Blue Swedish ducks
> 8 Indian runner ducks
> 150 Magpie ducks
> 150 Muscovy ducks (domestic stock)
> 200 Pekin ducks
> 202 Saxony ducks

Yes, someone had been on Wikipedia. I wasn't sure if Jason would be able to satisfy my duck-based needs. However, within just a few seconds he replied to say, 'No problem'. They must have a high-quality supply computer at Duck HQ – a bit like those little blue machines you get in Argos where you type in the code, and it tells you exactly how much stock they have behind the counter.

I didn't know who Jason was, but I couldn't thank him enough that he reached out on Instagram and was my new duck supplier. Of course, the issue with duck suppliers has always been delivery[14]. You can be waiting months for the delivery of ducks. So, I was very pleased when Jason stated his duck delivery deadlines.

> How quickly can you get me the 1,000 ducks?

 Now I can get it immediately

Jason was serious about supplying 1,000 ducks to me. So serious in fact, that he sent me many pictures of the ducks that she was going to send to me.

---

[14] That, and the bill. You didn't think we were going to do this chapter and not do that joke, did you?

We continued with our conversation. As you'd expect, I had quite a lot of question for Jason.

- Where do you get 1,000 ducks at short notice?
- Did you always wanted to be a duck wholesaler or was it something the Careers Advisor at school mentioned?
- Do you find your business strategy of messaging random people on Instagram is the best way to attract new customers?
- What is the name of your duck supplier business?

In relation to the last question, I told Jason I had some great names for his duck wholesaler business:

- Bills, Bills, Bills
- Don't Drake My Heart
- Alice in Swanderland

It seemed Jason was not in any mood for small talk.

 If you keep asking me questions bye

Jason provided more pictures of the ducks he had for sale.

Look at those cute little baby ducks! The issue was of course the payment. You don't have to have a GCSE in Math[15] to know that the total for this transaction was $50,000. Now, I didn't actually have $50,000, so I wanted to enquire if there might be the possibility of a discount for buying such a large quantity of mallards.

> Do you provide any sort of bulk buy duck discount?

Yes

This was great news. However, I was about to enter a very difficult and long negotiation process. I knew I had to be firm. I knew I had to be fair. The first rule of negotiation 'If you can avoid it - never make the first offer'. I set my stall out. I waited for Jason to move. Like a game of chess, we both had our kings protected. We both had knights that could move in funny directions. Finally, Jason moved flinched first and made the first move.

> So what is the total price with the bulk buy duck discount?

 Just pay me $1000 dollars

As bad at negotiating that I was, it seemed that Jason was 10 times worse. The original offer was for $50,000 and after Jason's counteroffer, it basically meant the deal was 'Buy 20 ducks, get 980 ducks free'.

It was the same approach for Berlins bar in Derby in 1998 where they offered the incredible deal of 'Buy 1 drink, get 3 drinks free'. An offer which led to many student nights out only costing about £6, but also being sick in the toilet, and back at home in bed by 8pm.

After a quick back and forth confirming the price, I could tell that Jason needed the money, and needed the money quick.

---

[15] s.

> Ok, so to confirm you have 1000 ducks ready waiting for me?

Yes I have

Jason was all business – and I respected him for that. We had agreed on the price, however there was still the issue on how I would receive the one thousand ducks to my home address.

It will be delivered to your door stop okay you don't need to worry it's my job

Just pay the $500 to my cashapp okay

This was all working out. I was so excited I very excitedly posted on Instagram about this incredible deal I was getting on the ducks. A friend got involved and wanted to know more, so I went back to Jason.

I have a friend who need 500 giraffes. Can you sort this too?

Make the payment

Wtf is wrong with you ?

Erm, nothing. I'm actually trying to get you some extra business. You would think that Jason would be pleased with this possible extra revenue, but he seemed a little perturbed.

We're trying to do a business deal and you talk to me like this

I already know what to do

I said make your payment

So I can deliver it

And you keep saying shit

Are you playing with me here

I was annoyed with the tone that Jason was using. Perhaps he was annoyed with himself for being so bad at negotiating – but there's no reason for him to take it out on me. I had to explain that this was not personal and was purely business – and she had to leave her emotions at the door.

I spoke to Jason about the importance of customer service and five-star Etsy reviews. I told him it could make or break his business. Eventually, Jason understood.

This is a business

I'm sorry

Thanks Jason, I appreciate it. I went back to the J-Dog and told him that I accepted his apology. He thanked me for this, and it seemed our business relationship was back on.

Now... can you get me 500 giraffes?

This may have been one order too many.

I don't do business this way

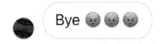 Bye 😠 😠 😠

Jason and I had a long conversation about how to conduct oneself during business a potential business transaction. It was getting pretty frosty between us to be honest, and I wondered if he was going to redact her offer of the 500 ducks.

Abnormal human being

Fuvk you ugly bitch

You broke ass you don't have money and you want to buy duck

I couldn't stay mad at Jason. Post pandemic, it's a difficult time to open a business. There's a cost-of-living crisis affecting us all, delivery costs are rising. However, I knew that keeping this relationship professional was the best way to go and I truly believed our business transaction would conclude. I, however, had one more thing to say to Jason.

I have one word for you

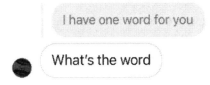 What's the word

Sorry, Jason.

Alaye

I used the Nigerian scamming term – 'Alaye' – a word from the Yoruba language, notifying the account holder that I knew he was a scammer. We'll look at some of these Yoruba words later on. He came back in some Yoruba (which I did not understand) and then asked me why I'd allowed him to use up all his data wasting his time on me.

Sorry, my bad.

Then he blocked me. Ducking hell.

**SEX**

Yes, a chapter called 'Sex'. Now, we all know that sex sells – and of course sex is one of the factors that scammers will use to get you to part with your money. Many a time I have had the following conversation with a scammer:

Scammer: Where are you from?
Me: UK
Scammer: OMG, I am in your country.
Me: Wow! OMG!
Scammer: Do you want to hook up and have sex?
Me: OMG! Totes yes.
Scammer: Where shall we meet?
Me: Have you heard of 5* hotel, Travelodge at Stansted?
Scammer: Yes baby
Me: OK – see you there in one hour.
Scammer: Oh no – I don't have enough gas to get to the hotel. Can you give me half the dollars I need, so we can have sex.
Me: Erm, what about your carbon footprint babe? Sure, I can't wait for sweet lovemaking, but we need to think of the planet babe (attaches bus and train timetables for Stansted Express)
Me (after no reply): Hello?
Me: (still no reply) You there hun?
Me: (still no reply) It actually works out cheaper if you get an EasyRider ticket. It just means you can hop on and hop off any time you like.
Me: (still no reply) Yeah, I'm still talking about the bus.
Me: (still no reply) Wazzzzzzzzup.

Anyway, this is Dorathy.

dorathywebb40    Following ∨

1 post    43 followers    105 following

Dorathy

Dorathy sent me a DM and used the word 'sex' three times in one sentence. I have never seen that before or since. She must know that sex sells. She knows what she's doing.

> I'm Dorathy I'm a sex worker I'm here to satisfy your sex urge and give you the best sex you ever had

 Are you interested

Let me have a think.

I told Dorathy I was indeed interested in her sexy proposal. To her credit, I appreciated that Dorathy used the term 'sex worker' instead of 'prostitute' (#2023 innit) but I didn't appreciate she spelt her name 'Dorathy'. Lots of red squiggly lines on Microsoft Word whilst writing this chapter[16].

I also appreciated her that she was very much up front with her offering and prices for the services she provided.

> $50 for normal hook up you can only Fuck,Suck, Kiss
>
> $100 for no limit one and half hour
>
> You can fuck the way you want too no limit
>
> $150 for a whole night you can also fuck the way you want it no limit

Like the menu at Nando's, it deserved a detailed inspection, so you know exactly what you're getting. It's too bad the pound is performing so badly against the dollar.

---

[16] Talking of Microsoft, what size shirt does a Microsoft spreadsheet wear? Excel.

I made my choice. It was a bit like the wine menu at a fancy restaurant. You don't want to appear to act like a cheap skate, so I opted for the second one down.

 Where do u want us to meet

Lassiters in Erinsborough

However, although it said I could *'fuck the way you want it no limit'* – I needed to put down a few ground rules – just so we both know we're on the same page. I had a few questions, and I needed answers to these questions before I handed over my $100.

Do you do spitback?

 I do squirt

Do you do French Swizzle?

 Yes

Full disclosure – I have no idea what 'French Swizzle' is. I also have no idea what 'Spitback' is[17].

But I was so very impressed that Dorathy does the French Swizzle! I wonder what other made-up sexy time analogies she does. I had to find out.

---

[17] They possibly supported Kings of Leon in 2005.

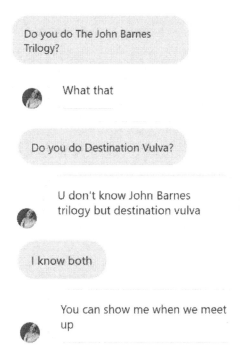

Do you do The John Barnes Trilogy?

What that

Do you do Destination Vulva?

U don't know John Barnes trilogy but destination vulva

I know both

You can show me when we meet up

Quite obviously, things were getting pretty spicy between Dorathy and I. Very spicy. Tesco Finest prawn madras spicy. I wanted to continue to find out what other sexy things she knew, and what things I would have to teach her.

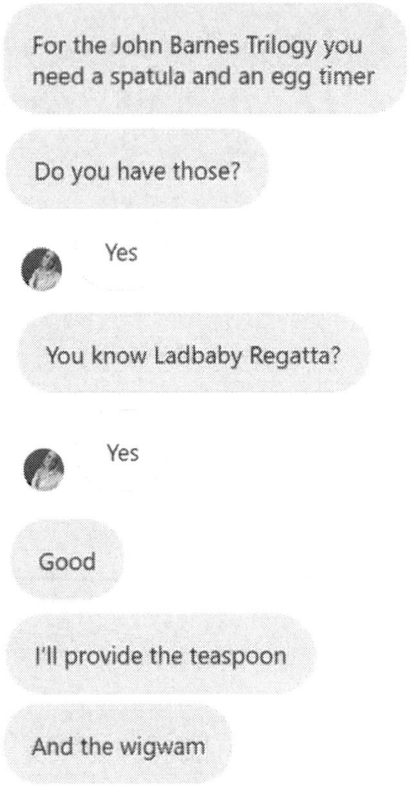

For the John Barnes Trilogy you need a spatula and an egg timer

Do you have those?

Yes

You know Ladbaby Regatta?

Yes

Good

I'll provide the teaspoon

And the wigwam

There was going to be a lot going on. Especially as I only had 60 minutes. I was also wearing a pair of trousers with a faulty zip, which could take a couple of minutes off proceedings.

I wondered if I had bit off more than I could chew. It was a bit like when you arrive at the all-you-can-eat Chinese buffet and you fill your first plate so high you need planning permission from the local council. It seemed Dorathy had the same concerns.

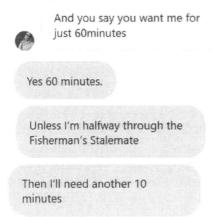

And you say you want me for just 60minutes

Yes 60 minutes.

Unless I'm halfway through the Fisherman's Stalemate

Then I'll need another 10 minutes

After a few more sexy terms (we agreed on three sessions of 'Ceefax Kissing', two portions of 'Hologram Reach Around' and one round of 'The Hulk Hogan Blowback') we settled on a time and location. It was clear that Dorathy was up for anything – but ruddy heck, she wanted paying.

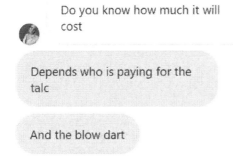

Do you know how much it will cost

Depends who is paying for the talc

And the blow dart

Well, it was agreed. We had a plan. Dorathy and I were going to be making sweet love. We agreed the location. We agreed the price. There was just one question that needed to be answered?

And who will film the sex?

We gonna set the camera ourselves

We only had 60 minutes. I can't be wasting time setting up cameras. Although, let's hope that Dorathy had some tripod experience. Am I right, guys?! Luckily, I had a back-up plan.

My mother is good at filming

 Lol your mom

Yes she's got a degree from the University of Stafford for photography and filmmaking

First of all – a little bit childish of Dorathy there with the 'Lol your mom' reference but I forgave her. We agreed (well, I sort of insisted) in the end that due to the expertise in the area, my mother could come along and film Dorathy and I making love.

Did Dorathy and I actually meet up and make love? Well, it's fair to assume we didn't. I quite incessantly kept talking about how the University of Staffordshire has an excellent reputation for an abundance of media courses and many graduates from the University of Staffordshire have gone on to great things in the media including being a Runner on the set of Going for Gold and Assistant Grip[18] on Birds of a Feather.

Because of my incessant talking about the merits of the University of Staffordshire, Dorathy questioned if I was mad, and then blocked me. That's 60 minutes and $100 saved I suppose. At least I didn't have to buy another wigwam.

---

[18] Possibly a service Dorathy offers.

**EVERYONE NEEDS GOOD NEIGHBOURS**

This is Kenny Brown. Despite having the name of a man, Kenny has the profile picture of an attractive woman. But don't let that put you off.

Kennybrown4246 follows 4,608 people, and she's specifically reaching out to me – I did feel very special. After going back and forth, Kenny asked me what I was on Instagram for – what my purpose was. Kenny said the reason she was on Instagram was because she offered a hook-up service and told me in no uncertain terms, she I was willing to have 'good time' in exchange for a certain amount of American dollars.

I told Kenny that sadly I was uninterested and that I was searching for somebody called Tina Tellison. I told her Tina was an old girlfriend of mine, and I was on Instagram to help search for her.

Kenny asked why I was trying to find her, and I said it was because I owed her money, and I needed to get the money to her. Kenny's nose pricked up at that news and asked how much I owed her and could I send a picture of Tina. I said I owed Tina £2,000, and I sent Kenny a picture of Tina Tellison.

Is it a bird? Is it a plane? No, it's Anne Haddy! The former Helen Daniels from BBC/Channel 5/no channel as of writing/ Australian soap opera, Neighbours. The chances of Kenny knowing Tina were slim. Very slim. But in the world of Instagram, you just never know…

I know her too

What?! What were the chances? Pretty small you would say! I couldn't believe my luck. It seemed that Kenny knew Tina and was more than happy to help me look for her. It would only cost me a small fee too.

What will you afford me if I get you her number to speak with her

To be sure though, Kenny asked for another photo of Tina. I was more than happy to oblige.

To help hunt for Tina, Kenny asked me a number of questions. I'd hoped by giving Kenny the answers, she would be able to tell me where Tina was.

Where did you meet her for the first place

In a lovely hotel complex called Lassiters

Now, we all know that it's been a while since our good friend Anne Haddy had been on our screens, and I told Kenny that the last time I'd spoken to Tina was 1993. Kenny didn't seem to mind that. However, she did deliver some bad news about the health status of Tina.

Right now as am speaking with
you now she's in the hospital

Oh no! Tina/Anne Haddy/Helen Daniels from Neighbours is in the hospital. I
was worried. Kenny told me that Tina had been in the hospital for over two
weeks. She said she knew Tina as she was the godmother of one of her friends.
She asked if I was going to come and visit her in the hospital. I told her I was
too busy, but a couple of friends would visit instead.

Des will come see her

Des and Daphne

However, the truth was I didn't want Tina to get better. I secretly wanted Tina
to snuff it. Kick the bucket. Meet her maker. Bite the big one. Check in to the
Horizontal Hilton. I know, how rude of me. I asked Kenny a question that would
change our relationship forever.

Can you kill her for me??

Kenny was obviously confused. Instantly, she replied back with 'Why?'. But
there was only one reason I wanted her dead.

So I can be sent the body and I
can eat her

You'd think that this kind of message would scare and put a stranger off. It
didn't put Kenny off. Although she seemed a little confused, she was happy to
continue with this silly charade.

 Can you please tell me what's
going on with you and her

Erm Kenny – I think it's pretty obvious. Me and the Ramsey Street Renegades

27

want Tina/Anne Haddy/Helen Daniels from Neighbours dead so we can eat her rotten corpse. I mean, how difficult is that to understand?

> Replied to you
>
> So Paul Robinson will see

 Who's Paul Robinson

Paul Robinson and Karl Kennedy are going to watch me eat her

Kenny seemed confused. To be fair, rightfully so.

 Can you eat dead body

Me, Paul and Karl will

Susan Kennedy doesn't approve

Sadly for Kenny, she didn't seem to realise we were talking about the residents of Ramsey Street. Over the course of thirty minutes, I reeled off a number of Ramsey Street regulars and even some peripheral characters[19] to keep Kenny informed of what we planned to do. She was getting suspicious and confused.

 Why you asking?

They are all in this

To eat the dead body

---

[19] Stonefish Rebecchi anyone?!

This was turning into quite an interesting Saturday afternoon. Here I was, pretending to be a woman who was searching for another fictional person who looked exactly like Helen Daniels, so we could eat her, whilst talking to a Nigerian scammer, who was also pretending to be a woman called Kenny.

Kenny seemed unsure.

> Please can you tell me what's
> really going on

I retold the story to Kenny, and asked her if she knew Mrs Mangle, Toadie, Todd Landers, Brad Willis or Madge Bishop. I explained that here in Erinsborough, we had a pact. When one of us dies, the rest of the neighbourhood eats that person. It's just part of our culture. It's our tradition. I explained when one of the residents dies, we place their body on a spit, and as they cook, we all sing a song to our departed Ramsey Street resident.

> Neighbours
> Everybody needs good
> neighbours
> With a little understanding
> you can find the perfect blend
>
> Neighbours should be there for
> one another
> That's when good neighbours
> become good friends

I had a bit of a sense that Kenny was a getting a little freaked out with my words.

> Bouncer is barking
>
> Mrs Mangel is howling
>
> I think it's time

Hmm I think you really serious

Despite being freaked out, there was an opportunity for Kenny the Nigerian scammer to make some money. Kenny could charge me for 'killing' Tina and make some serious sweet, sweet coin. I started haggling with Kenny to agree a price on bumping off Tina.

We went back and forth on the price to kill Tina. I started with the offer of $5,000.

Despite offering $5,000 to kill, Kenny wasn't having any of it. She wanted more. Her haggling skills were impressive.

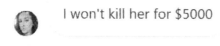

$7,000 to kill an old woman? It seemed pretty steep to me. I thought I should shop around and see if I could get the hit done for less money.

I went on to the dark web[20] to try to find another assassin who could get the job done for me at a better price. The great news about being on the dark web is that you never have to accept cookies and there are very few pop-up adverts.

---

[20] wwww.darkweb.com (yeah, it's 4 W's).

Say what you like about the dark web, but it hasn't been hugely affected by GDPR.

Anyway, the good news was I found someone willing to kill Tina at what I believed was a bargain price.

This man has offered to do it for $6800

He has offered $6800. His name is Lou Carpenter

I don't think that Kenny thought she was going to be in a bidding war. But sadly, when you are shelling out muchos honk for an assassination, you have to shop around.

 Sorry why is he offered money to kill her

I put an advert on the internet and he responded

Ohh really

The haggling was becoming quite a long and laborious process. I now understand why all these politicians negotiate throughout the night for those amazing Brexit deals we got[21]. In the end, Kenny decided she wanted to

---

[21] Hmmm.

communicate on another platform to continue the negotiation.

 Sorry do you have hangout?

Is it more secure? I'm concerned we are planning a murder on here

The password is 'Murder Murder Let's Plan The Murder'

Kenny and I chatted a bit more on the upcoming murder, and I let her know how we were also excited for this to happen.

Paul Robinson says hello

He's only got one leg

Kenny had had enough and blocked me. This was a big shame, as I was hoping we would become great friends and maybe even live next door to each other.

*That's when good neighbours become good friends.*

## ROSE MERRY

Let me introduce you to my new Instagram friend Rose Merry. Actually, I will let Rose do that. She introduces herself by saying 'Hi' and accompanies that greeting with a picture of her clacker.

Hi

It turns out that Rose Merry was only after one thing – sex! You heard me – sex! And by sex, I mean she wants me to give her money for sex, and then not turn up to have sex, and keep the money for themselves.

A little rascal. Oh, and by 'she', I mean 'scammer'. Well, I had to get to the (front) bottom of it. Turns out she charges $200 for an hour of sex. Which does seem like a lot of money. But, as it turns out, there are some positives...

It's seems quite a lot for an hour of sex (minus taking my big trousers off)

Do you provide tea and biscuits after?

 Yes

So, at least you get a Typhoo and Hobnob afterwards. After a brief conversation from me about the time it takes to take my big trousers off, Rose Merry hit me with a conversation starter which I returned with a Salt-n-Pepa reference which flew over her head.

 Let's talk about sex

baby... let's talk about you and me

After more deliberation, including Rose Merry sending some very nude photos (not shown), we agreed on what we would do (sex) a date (the date of sex) and a time (time of sex) and a place of sex (vagina). We'd also agreed on the $200 fee, and it was decided that Rose Merry would come to my house for this event.

This led me to my first problem. Not wanting to give my real address away, I had to provide a false residence and hope that Rose Merry didn't realise that it was a fake.

221b Baker Street, London

Yup, I had agreed to meet a fictional person at the home of Sherlock Holmes. As you may know, this address is actually a very bad place to have sex, because there is no bedding at the residence. No sheet, Sherlock[22].

It turns out that Rose Merry lives in Greenwich, just a few miles away from the fictional address I had given, so nothing could go wrong. We agreed she would come over at 4pm, so we would be all finished to watch Tipping Point[23].

In the beginning of our dalliance, Rose Merry had been all about wanting to nob me, but after agreeing to this, all she seemed even more interested in buying her a gift card, and to be honest, it was killing the mood.

> Can you send me a gift card to come

 Now

> This isn't very sexy talk Rose

I had to get Rose back on to the subject of nobbing me.

> Tell me what you'll do if I get you the gift card

OK I want to fuck you

Much better Rose, much better. I was determined to make sure that I got my hour of sexy time with Rose Merry.

---

[22] I make no apologies for that joke.
[23] After she saw my tipping point, am I right?!

Can I do weird stuff?

Like spit in your handbag?

Trace your shins and save them to my desktop

Try and make bread in the shape of your thorax

Rose agreed to these unconventional requests, and we were all set for 4pm. I could hardly control myself. I showered and cleaned most of my zones and I was all ready for Rose. Well, 4pm came and went and guess what... Rose didn't turn up (no shit, Sherlock). I mean, to be fair – she might have turned up – I just wasn't at Baker Street to let her in. However, she got in contact, and we decided to rearrange.

 Should I come today

The Krypton Factor is on tonight

What about tomorrow?

 OK no problem

After we had rearranged our meeting when The Krypton Factor wasn't on and to keep the conversation going, I had no choice but to send Rose Merry what she asked for – an iTunes card.

Obviously, the image I sent was just some iTunes card I found on the internet and on closer inspection, it's all in German[24]. While Rose was checking the card was legit, I was busy getting prepared for an hour of great lovemaking.

I'm doing lunges in anticipation of you coming over

Just cleaning the flat

Having some a protein shake

Now a hobnob

I was getting ready for 60 minutes of a mild to intensive cardio workout and I knew the importance of fuelling for such an event.

---

[24] iTunes? NeinTunes more like!

Having some pasta

I'm carb loading

 That's good

And stretching

 I want to have sex and a lot of fun with you

Having some rice

Feeling sluggish now

Oh dear. Not only had I massively overloaded on complex carbohydrates, but it appeared Rose Merry was getting suspicious about the iTunes voucher I'd sent her. Could I keep getting away with these shenanigans?

OK when did you buy the card

The 8th

Or 10th

Not the 9th as I went to see my
friend Johnny Hulu on that day

Well, it turns out that Rose worked out the card had already been used, so
demanded that I get a new one. I said that would be fine, and within a few
minutes, I was back at the store to get a new card for her.

 Can I see a picture of you at the
store

Oh heck! I obviously wasn't at the store, so once again I went to Google images
to try to prove to Rose Merry where I was.

I know what you are thinking – do those chewing gums come free with any
purchase? No, they are Extra. As I was about to buy Rose a new gift card, I got a
phone call. I answered the call. It was bad news. I went straight back to
Instagram to tell Rose.

The hospital have just called. My mum has gone missing. She's walked out of the hospital and has gone missing

Yeah, things got pretty serious with my fictional mother being taken to a fictional hospital. To her credit, the fictional Rose Merry seemed pretty concerned about her, and not bothered about the iTunes voucher I promised I would get her. Despite my mother's illness, Rose still wanted to come over and give me nobbing.

 Should I come or not

It would be nice but I feel like I won't be in the mood

Oh I will seduce you that you will be in the mood

I loved rose's attitude here. Yes, my soon to be lover has just heard the news his mother has been taken ill and rushed to hospital. You know what would cheer him up? Thirty minutes of gland to gland combat.

I was adamant that I had other things on my mind, and I had to focus on my mother, so I would be travelling to the hospital to be by her side. However, I told Rose I had got a 'Get Well Soon' card for my sick mum and asked what message she would like to put in it from her.

What message shall I put in there from you?

Just tell her that's she will get better

Which type of card will you get for me

Typical isn't it... you mention 'cards' and suddenly, she's back on me buying the bloody iTunes card. Anyway, today is not about you Rose, it's about my sick mother. However, it was important that I put a message from Rose in the card – and show my mum that her child and special lady were thinking of her on her road to recovery.

I've put 'don't worry, you'll get better. From Rose Merry' on the card

Is that ok?

That didn't quite sit right.

I've put 'don't worry little petal , you'll get better. You are the best mum in law ever. Love from Rose Merry, your future daughter in law. I'm really good at sucking dick and riding dick' on the card. Is that ok?

Yes baby

 I love that

Perfect! We got there in the end, and Rose seemed to be happy with it. It looked like today was going to be a good day after all. But then... suddenly, I had to give her some awful news.

The hospital have just called. My mum has gone missing. She's walked out of the hospital and has gone missing

No! My poor frail fictional mother. I wondered how our scammer would reply to this very serious event.

Oh sorry that's hurt

 Can I see the picture of your mum

That's a good idea.

Is it so you can help look for her?

I was so pleased that Rose and I were on the same page when it came to this. Rose was concerned and she seemed OK to hunt for my mother around Greenwich while I look for her around the ... 'Sherlock Holmes area' of London.

The only issue is that I now had to send a picture of my fictional mother. So, on to Google I went and imaged *'old frail woman'*. Hey Preston (sic), my fictional mother was born!

And there began the adventure of two people both posing as fictional characters beginning a search for another fictional person across the great city of London.

But no matter how much I told Rose about my sick mother, it seemed she would always come back to talk about wanting this gift card.

I'm in west London looking

Just go and get the card for me now and I will make sure I looked for her and get her back

I have to find my mum first. That is more important than your steam card

We searched and we searched, but alas we could not find my sick, frail mother.

How was this story end? Rose sent me a message and sent the story into another direction entirely.

If you can get me the card you
will See your mom

Er, what? Say again?

How do you know? Do you
know where mum is?

Yes

Cue the Eastenders music! What?! What was going on? How did Rose Merry know where my frail, sick imaginary mother was? Why hadn't she told me? Was my mother OK? Was the woman behind the counter at the newsagents really wearing mittens? I had so many questions – but it appeared that for some reason, Rose Merry, the very woman that I just about to get jiggy with, had kidnapped my mother!

Oh my god

Where is she?

I will go and get her now

Just get me the card first

Rose was blackmailing me! I couldn't believe it! We were (soon to be) lovers just minutes before, and now she is holding my poor, frail mother hostage until she receives an iTunes card?! Well, I had seen the 1996 action movie Ransom, I knew what was going on here. There was only one thing for it...

> (Says in a Mel Gibson voice) ...
> Give me back my mum!

The ball was in my court if I wanted to see my fictional family member again. I wanted my sick, frail mother back. Rose Merry wanted money. This was a hostage situation. I hate hostage negotiations. I hate the bit where you eventually get to the counter and haggle with someone about the fee of sending a letter to Scotland. No, hang on, that's postage negotiations.

> Do you have my mum hostage ?

> Huge development if true

> Yes

> But get the card now and get
> back your mom

I was scared. Shocked. Angry. Alone. Do I call the police? The FBI? Shaw Taylor from Police 5? All I know is that I desperately wanted my mum back, and I was going to do anything to do it. Apart from buy a scammer an iTunes voucher though obvs. I had to think. What do they do in the movies when someone gets kidnapped? Yes, I knew exactly what to do!

> I need proof of life.

> Please send a photo of my mum

Proof of life! Do bear in mind that just a few short hours ago, she was lying in a hospital bed. What an ordeal she's been through! But on the other side of this, the scammer has now got to provide proof of life for a fictitious old lady. What will they do? This is what they sent.

Yes, the scammer had just resent the same photo I had sent them. But man alive, scammer – please charge your phone, you're making me nervous over here!

I asked Rose if she'd given my mum the insulin she desperately needed every six hours to keep her blood/sugar level at a manageable level. She said she had.

I asked Rose if she had given my mum the Sanatogen she desperately needs every day to make sure her vitamin D levels are suitably managed. She said she had.

I asked Rose if she had cancelled the badminton class my mother had got booked for Monday evening with her friend Shuttlecock Sheila. She told me to shut up and stop asking so many questions.

I was trying my hardest for Rose Merry to provide proof of life to my mother.

What is her favourite song?
Please ask her

She did not tell me

Rose told me that she was alive though, and I had to take her word for it. I just couldn't take it anymore. I had to get my mother back. But do you know what? Despite this kidnapping business, there was still a sexual frisson between Rose Marie and me. Just something in the air (maybe it was the smell from the first photo she sent me). I wish we could put this whole kidnapping business behind us and carry on like we were before. Rose seemed to agree.

> You will release my mother that you have taken hostage and then you will have sex with me?

> Yes

It did feel like a sexy Stockholm Syndrome was occurring right before our eyes. But then, after all this – the news I was dreading finally arrived. Maybe it was the fact that I was asking too many questions. Maybe it was the fact I was asking for photos of the inside of my mother's mouth so I could confirm it was her due to the number of fillings she had. I don't know what pushed Rose over the edge. But I obviously went too far.

 I kill her already

Numb. I was numb. How could she do this? My fictional mother! I will never get over this. Between the tears and the wailing, I had to find out what her final words were.

> What were her final words?

 She said you will never survive in your life

Typical final words from my mum! She's never forgiven me for taping over that Christmas episode of Taggart – 'A Murder Amongst the Mince Pies' in 1994. I calmed my nerves; my fingers were still shaking. But I sent an image to Rose Merry that just summed up the whole situation.

Rose Merry replied back with a question that surprised me.

 Should we have sex today

Yes, I was in mourning. Yes, I was upset that Rose had kidnapped and then murdered my mother. But God damn, I was still well up for some saucy Rose Merry action (as well as a hobnob and cuppa).

However, sadly that's where the adventure ended. It was apparent that the person behind Rose Merry realised they weren't going to get any iTunes cards from me. There was silence from Rose. There was silence from me. Our relationship was over. No hobnobs. No sex. No Typhoo. We were left with more questions than that we knew we weren't going to get answers from – such as, why was the woman at the newsagent really wearing mittens?

Despite my many questions to Rose, she ignored them all. A couple of days later, I got a message from Rose out of the blue.

 I don't kill your mom

She was just joking! I know, big lols! What a practical joker. She's like a millennial Jeremy Beadle.

Rose Merry then blocked me.

I wondered if the scammer had had as much fun as I did riding this emotional scam-based rollercoaster and at what point they'd realised this was all for a lost cause. Maybe the scammer was with his Nigerian friends, all wondering where the next part of the story was coming from. Maybe one of them asked

'*Kini idi ti iyaafin yẹn ni ile itaja wọ awọn ibọwọ*' – which translates from Yoruba as 'Why was that woman in the shop wearing mittens?'

In real life, my real-life mum doesn't look anything like my fictional mother. As silly as a lot of these stories are, my real-life mum has some great stories herself. Around 20 years ago, there was a big murder court case in Stafford and my mum decided to go to the public gallery and watch the entire case, which lasted a few weeks. Every couple of days I would call her to ask how the trial was going, and every time she would talk about the defendant. 'Guilty!' she was shout down the phone at me. 'The man is guilty. You can tell by his eyes. He's always writing notes down as well. This guy is a sicko' she'd say.

The next week was the same. 'Lock him up James, the man is scum. His eyes. He's showing no remorse either, just scribbling down words on some paper throughout. My skin runs cold when I see him'. The following week I called her and asked how if the defendant is still acting strange. She told me she'd got the wrong guy and she had been eyeballing the journalist from The Staffordshire Sentinel.

Love you mum.

**SUSAN SMITH**

The dialogue that scammers use is always quite similar. They will always ask you where you are from. Once you have given your country, by some incredible miraculous coincidence – it turns out that they are from the same country as you. Many conversations will be as blunt as this.

*'Hi. How are you?'*
*'Hello'*
*'Where are you from?'*
*'UK'*
*'Wow – me too! I am available for hook up. Fancy some fun hun?'*[25]

The wonderful Susan Smith messaged me and asked where I was from. After saying I lived I London, it turned out that she lived in London too. She then gave her address to me.

21 Saville Rd

That's my address

We are close

Oh, we were close indeed. Really close. Because I gave Susan the big revelation.

I'm at 23 Saville Road!

We're neighbours!

It's not often you message a stranger, and you suddenly realise that instead of messaging someone on the other side of the world, they are actually just

---

[25] chick/love/babe/lan

behind the dividing wall. What a happy coincidence this was. Susan seemed happy with it too.

Wow 😄 cool

Can you come over for sex fun

Here we bloody go! Actual sex! With an actual woman! I couldn't believe it. My wildest dreams were about to come true, with Susan at number 21! If this was 2001, and the 22-year-old virgin James Billington[26] would be putting his best bootcut jeans on, drowning himself in Lynx Java[27] and knocking on number 21 as soon as possible. But now I was a more mature person. Who was I kidding? I put my bootcut jeans[28] on and got ready to go next door.

My mind was going wild with all the minutes of missionary sex we were going to do. The good news was I had nothing to do that day. All I had planned was to watch the latest Tom Cruise movie where he attempts to have sex with heavily obese women[29]. My reply to Susan bordered on needy.

Let me come over and say hello

See you in 2 minutes

It was enough time to grab some of the stuff you need for sexy times: prophylactic x 2, custard creams x 2 and The Joy of Sex manual x 1. I grabbed my stuff, and I was just about to leave the house when Susan replied again.

---

[26] I was waiting for the right person, OK?
[27] Do scammers in Africa use Lynx Europe?
[28] They're back in fashion guys.
[29] Missionary Impossible

When coming help me get a
game card

For my nephew

 At the store

Susan wanted me to get her a game card on the way to her house. Erm, babe I'm next door! Babe, the nearest store is a 10-minute walk – get it yourself after we've done nobbing each other! Well, it didn't take me long to get my shoes on and head over to Susan's house.

I'm here already

I'm knocking on your door

Answer the door

Nothing could go wrong. Nothing. I was on a promise, and I was going to enjoy both minutes of it.

 My dad is around

Oh. Well, this was a bit of an issue. What about the moaning, the screaming and the 'YES YES YES!'. Well, I was just going to have to keep my voice down. Never mind, I was sure this wouldn't be an issue. And, just like that I told her what was happening.

A man is coming to the door

I will explain to him that I'm here
to have sex with Susan smith

I was looking forward to Susan's father and exchanging British pleasantries with him before getting some afternoon delight with his daughter. Weirdly though, Susan seemed to get a bit reluctant.

Are you mad

Or crazy

I'm not sure why Susan was being so coy. She was the one that had invited me round for sexual shenanigans and yet now I was at her front door[30]. Whilst I was checking my Instagram messages, a figure appeared at the door. As the figure got closer, I started to make out a few of their features.

Slowly the door became unlocked, and the door opened. I quickly took a photo of the man at the door and sent it to Susan.

Susan seemed confused.

It appeared the gentlemen was not Susan's father. This was a little confusing. I had the right address. So, who was the gentlemen and what was he doing in

---

[30] Not a euphemism

the house of Susan Smith?

> That's not my address

> You are crazy

I'm here talking to an old man

Susan was acting a little odd. Not only was her English becoming more ineligible and occasionally using words I didn't understand, but I just couldn't understand why there was a stranger at her house. Susan, however, had an answer.

> I live in the next street

> Heath Gardens

It is sometimes difficult when you live at 'Heath Gardens', you do occasionally type that address as 'Saville Road'. Fair play to the scammer though, he was doing his best at this point. He was obviously on Google Maps looking at roads adjoining Saville Road in London — and Heath Gardens popped up. For those interested, Heath Gardens is the adjacent street to Saville Road in Twickenham, London. Back to the story — I was not going to just say bye to this elderly gentleman I had just met.

This guy is lovely. His name is Peter. He's retired

He makes a great cup of tea and he's offered me battenburg

Peter and I were getting on like a house on fire. We had a lot in common. We'd both lost our virginity at 22, we both could only name three members of boyband Blue and we'd both stopped watching The Bill when DI Burnside left the show.

He'd also offered me my favourite type of cake too. What a legend he was. However, Susan was becoming more and more impatient with the events unfolding in front of her.

... Peter is really nice by the way

Did you know his granddaughter plays piano for the backing group that go on tour with The Magic Numbers?

It appeared that Susan wasn't a fan of Peter, and sadly didn't appear to be a fan of 00's pop band The Magic Numbers.

Don't ever text me again

Right we're off to bingo now and a chippy dinner

And with that Susan blocked me. Sadly, we will never know if Susan (not her real name) lived at Heath Gardens (she doesn't) or Saville Road (she doesn't) or if deep down, she really was a fan of The Magic Numbers. Susan was Forever Lost[31].

---

[31] Forever Lost was The Magic Number's second biggest hit. No, I didn't know either.

## FAMOUS FACES

officialkeanucharlesreeves9...   Message

0 posts    505 followers    872 following

K C R
President of company 3 Arts Entertainment,Inc. based in Beverly hills, CA. Film producer
IF YOU FOLLOW ME BACK PLEASE TEXT ME OK I'LL RESPOND BACK....
www.3art.com

Let's move on to the famous faces scam! The celebrity scam. Celebrities have Instagram too! It also makes you feel great when you get an email from a celebrity. I mean, who wouldn't want a direct message from Birds of a Feather actress, Pauline Quirke[32]? You may not know this, but sometimes celebrities only have 12 followers on Instagram. Sure, they might be multi-millionaire movie stars, have luxury apartments all over the world, be regularly featured on the cover of More magazine[33], but even they struggle to amass more than 12 followers on certain social media platforms. Yes, I'm looking at you Keanu Reeves.

I don't know what it is about Keanu Reeves, but I have had eight different fake Keanu Reeves accounts contacting me. I don't know why Keanu Reeves is such a character for contacting random people on social media, asking strangers:

a) If they are a big fan of them
b) If they've seen any of their movies
c) Asking for $300 to update their computer software.

You'd think he might have the funds to do that himself, but apparently, he doesn't have enough signal to do the transaction when filming John Wick 4. But he does have enough signal to message me.

Sadly, it also appears that these celebrities have a pretty poor grasp of the English language. Over the last 18 months, I have had conversations with multiple Mark Zuckerberg's, WWE superstars Charlotte Flair and Liv Morgan, Meghan Markle and multiple members of the band BTS.

I once had a lovely conversation with Sylvester Stallone who told me what his hobbies were.

---

[32] Linda Robson?
[33] Anyone else miss 'Position of the Fortnight'?

Sylvester Stallone  25 Apr at 18:35
my hobby are watching movies, cooking,
going for walks, listening to music
(almost,all types of music), singing,
reading, surfing the internet love
shopping and I also love to swim?

Good to know that Sly enjoys surfing the internet and listens to (almost) all
types of music. With my interactions with all these celebrities, it's been sad to
see that being a celebrity doesn't mean you have a life of riches and glamour. It
can sometimes mean you message random strangers on Instagram and through
broken English, ask for iTunes vouchers. Let's look at Keanu Reeves then.

**WHO IS THE REAL KEANU?**

It's amazing when you get an interaction from an actual celebrity, isn't it? Whether that's a tweet from Big Brother winner Craig Phillips, maybe you've been tagged in a Facebook photo with Timothy Spall, or you get a restraining order from Lisa Scott Lee.

On this occasion, I was absolutely flabbergasted to get a message on Instagram from Hollywood movie star Keanu Reeves. The actual Keanu Reeves obviously. I knew it was the real Keanu Reeves because the profile picture of Keanu Reeves was a picture of Keanu Reeves holding a piece of paper where he'd written the words 'I am tired of explaining to people that I am Keanu Reeves. This is my only page'.

I think it must be difficult for Keanu Reeves making people believe that he is the real Keanu Reeves, and not some fake Keanu Reeves, pretending to be Keanu Reeves. That's the reason why the real Keanu Reeves, and not a charlatan Keanu Reeves, has done what only Keanu Reeves could do, and taken a photo of him (Keanu Reeves) with a piece of paper saying 'I am tired of explaining to people that I am Keanu Reeves. This is my only page'. Well played Keanu Reeves. Well played.

## Keanu Reeves

keanureeves29656 · Instagram

It was fascinating to me just why there was so many Keanu Reeves impersonators on Instagram. All of them pretending to be this Hollywood A-lister. It turns out that you cannot complain to Instagram and report that fake Keanu Reeves is pretending to be the real Keanu Reeves... because the real Keanu Reeves isn't on Instagram at all. Therefore, you can't impersonate someone who isn't there!

I typed in 'Keanu Reeves' on the search function within Instagram. There were dozens of accounts. Dozens of scammers, all pretending to be this Hollywood star. Dozens of people trying to convince people all over the world that they were the leading face in the Bill and Ted franchise.

So, it was a wonderful delight to get a direct message from the real Keanu Reeves telling me that he was indeed the real Keanu Reeves (obviously he was, I hadn't at any point considered he wasn't the real Keanu Reeves) and that it was great to interact with his fans. Keanu Reeves asked me if I was a fan of his work and if I had seen all of the movies he had starred in. I explained that I was indeed a fan of his work, and I had probably seen around 20% of his movies.

It was really nice to see Keanu Reeves, and to be honest, he was just a regular guy. The kind of guy you see on the subway in America just minding his own business which makes for great content on Facebook. We had a lovely chat. He talked about how busy he was filming another movie, when all of a sudden, I got another Instagram message from ANOTHER Keanu Reeves! How was this possible? Was there a glitch in The Matrix?! I couldn't believe my eyeballs.

**kenue revess**

revesskenue · Instagram

15 followers · 5 posts

Well, it wasn't quite Keanu Reeves, he called himself *'kenue revees'*, but most of the letters were in the right place. He also said he was the real Keanu Reeves. To be fair to him, he looked like Keanu Reeves and he spoke like Keanu Reeves (if Keanu Reeves spoken in very broken English and said he needed iTunes vouchers to upgrade his computer).

I just couldn't believe that there were two Keanu Reeves's speaking to me at the same time. Obviously one[34] of them had to be a fake, and I really wanted to know which one that was. I was so confused. Both people were saying that they were the real Keanu Reeves, and it was extremely confusing. There was only one thing that I could do.

I decided to create a private Instagram chat between myself, Keanu Reeves 1 and Keanu Reeves 2 to find out who exactly was the real Keanu Reeves. Instead of asking them individually, I invited us all to have a mature discussion and find out the truth.

---

[34] Not two. That would be ridiculous.

# Who is the real Keanu Reeves?

Change name & photo

Like a millennium Columbo, I was going to find out who indeed was the real Keanu Reeves, and who was a mere charlatan.

> You're a both messaging me at the same time
>
> Who is the real Keanu Reeves?

Straightaway both Keanu Reeves's came back at me to tell me that they were the real Keanu Reeves.

'Keanu Reeves 1' was telling me that the FBI were involved in this. This mystery was now being dealt with by the lead federal agency for investigating cyber-attacks by criminals, overseas adversaries, and terrorists. It was exciting to be part of this. I wondered if I could solve this mystery before the FBI could, so I continued with my Roger Cook style investigative skills.

To help crack the case, I asked both Keanu Reeves's their date of birth. This was information that only the real Keanu Reeves would know and is certainly not information you could find out by asking a man called Jeeves.

kenue revess

> I was born on September 2nd
> 1964 I am 59 years old

Well, it seemed the mystery was over. 'Keanu Reeves 2' knew the birthday of Keanu Reeves, so I could only assume that he was the real Keanu Reeves. However, 'Keanu Reeves 1' told me another story.

Keanu Reeves

> I was born in September 2nd
> 1965 okay

Wait? What? 'Keanu Reeves 1' was telling he was born in 1965, whereas 'Keanu Reeves 2' was saying he was born in 1964. I was confused. So very confused. Whilst my head was spinning, both 'Keanu Reeves 1' and 'Keanu Reeves 2' started having an argument amongst themselves to say they were the real Keanu Reeves and that the other was a fake.

kenue revess

> This parson here is fake

> You don't know when you were
> born

Keanu Reeves

> I was not born 1964

kenue revess

> Stop pretending you are fake
> profile

It was all a bit too much if I'm honest. Here I was trying to enjoy my day when a real Keanu Reeves and a fake Keanu Reeves were arguing with each other about who was the real Keanu Reeves and who was the fake Keanu Reeves. The arguing continued.

I was not born 1964

You get that from Google you are fake profile

Keanu Reeves

Dear you can ask your Google okay I was born 1965 September second now I am 58 years old not 59 okay ask Google

It seemed that Google and the rest of the world wide web (dark included) knew the date of birth of Keanu Reeves, so there had to be another plan of action. What else could I do to help distinguish between these two Reeves's? Before I could do anything, 'Keanu Reeves 1' pulled out his passport and sent me a picture of it!

Well, that was surely the information I needed to finally put this mystery to bed. However, 'Keanu Reeves 2' had other ideas. He said that the passport was fake and there was only one thing to prove he was indeed the real Keanu.

kenue revess

Rasi you hand up were you are now

If you are real

For those of you who might need a little help on this, 'Rasi you hand up you are now' translates as 'Raise your hand up, wherever you are now'. I didn't think anything of this, until I got the following image from 'Keanu Reeves 2'.

kenue revess

So, 'Keanu Reeves 2' had sent me what he promised. A picture of him with his hand 'rasied' in the air. I was back to being in a Keanu Reeves based pickle. Where would this end? Was this getting silly? I'll let you be the judge of that after this quick back and forth.

I'm the real Keanu Reeves

I'm the real Keanu Reeves

I'm Spartacus

I felt like I was going round in circles. Even 'Keanu Reeves 1' said he was tired and wanted to sleep. I'm sorry 'Keanu Reeves 1', I had a case to solve, and I need you to help me solve this mystery. Fear not though reader, I had another way to help me. I asked both Keanu Reeves's how many Matrix movies there were. Again, this is information that Keanu Reeves and only Keanu Reeves would know.

Question: how many films of
The Matrix were there?

Keanu Reeves

 3 okay

 The: matrix
The: reloaded
The: revolutions

It seemed that 'Keanu Reeves 1' knew that there were three Matrix films and what's more he also knew the titles of them as well! When I did put it to 'Keanu Reeves 1' about 'The Matrix Resurrections' in 2021, his reply was wonderful.

Keanu Reeves

 Yes of course

If 'Keanu Reeves 1' could not name all the Matrix movies, then it surely meant that he was indeed the charlatan, and 'Keanu Reeves 2' was indeed the real Keanu Reeves. It seemed I had cracked the case. 'Keanu Reeves 2' took glee in the fact that 'Keanu Reeves 1' had tripped up in not knowing that there was a fourth Matrix movie, and that I appeared to believe him in thinking he was the Keanu Reeves. He even managed to give us both a little review of the latest Matrix film.

 Resurrection isn't really bad it
was watchable but has its
limitation

'Keanu Reeves 1' seemed to be scrambling a bit. Instead of trying to convince us as to who he was, he went on a rant talking about love, trust and all sorts of other things. It was the kind of rant that makes Russell Brand seem 'concise'.

i got you this letter for you to read and understand it well ok i want you to be thankful and happy that you finally met your dream woman while im doing the same here cos we are both in the state no game and no fake so please i want you to have a strong trust and feelings to me cos without trust in a relationship is nothing please try to learn how to trust from now cos i want us to settle down together and we need trust from the start ok ......

You need trust to love, but first you need to love in order to trust.To love someone is to understand each other, to laugh together, to smile with your heart and to trust one another. One important thing is to let each other go if you can't do this.Love is like a wonderful feeling of compassion and satisfaction. It should be given respect and trust; and it should receive that love back.The best proof of love is trust.]; but finding love and finding trust was a gift from you to me.Relationships should never be taken for granted.

'Keanu Reeves 1' was a very wise man, wasn't he?! 'You need trust to love, but first you need to love in order to trust'. Such wise words. At this point, both Keanu Reeves's continued to argue among themselves about the other person being fake, and they were the real Keanu Reeves. I had created a monster. I just sat back and listened. Every now and again I would just interject with some very silly comment that would stoke the fire even more.

The bickering continued. 'Keanu Reeves 1' and 'Keanu Reeves 2' were both bickering with each other about where the real Keanu Reeves was from? Was it America or Canada?

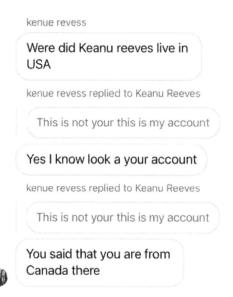

Both Keanu's kept messaging me privately to get the other Keanu blocked and to believe them that they were indeed the real Keanu Reeves. I told them both that the group chat is where we had to communicate and that is where we would find out the truth.

True to his word, 'Keanu Reeves 1' started talking about the FBI again. He'd had enough of 'Keanu Reeves 2' and he said that it was time to get the FBI involved to report what was going on. However, 'Keanu Reeves 2' wasn't having any of this. He was calling the other Keanu's bluff. This was getting pretty serious.

'Keanu Reeves 2' was pulling out the big guns on 'Keanu Reeves 1' — telling him to name the FBI Director without using the internet. If he was going to report the account to the FBI, surely he would know the name of the FBI Director? It was all getting a bit tense. And then, just out of nowhere.

'Keanu Reeves 2' had pulled it out of the bag! If you didn't know, Wikipedia shows *'Christopher Asher Wray (born December 17, 1966) is an American attorney who is the current director of the Federal Bureau of Investigation (FBI). He was nominated by President Donald Trump on June 7, 2017, and has served since August 2, 2017.'*

How would 'Keanu Reeves 1' respond to this? The ball was in his court, and he had to pull out all the stops here. The one thing I have learned through this very silly conversation was that you should never, ever, underestimate 'Keanu Reeves 1'.

Can you tell me ten people on FBI

Name 10 people from the FBI? It was a heck of an ask. Could I name 10 people from the FBI? Obviously, there's Mulder and Scully – that's two. Clarice from The Silence of the Lambs. Sandra Bullock from the Miss Congeniality movies. That's only four FBI-ians. I couldn't even name 10 people from FBI. How would 'Keanu Reeves 2' respond to this?

Well, he couldn't. Now it was 'Keanu Reeves 2' turn to say he was tired of this. It was indeed pretty exhausting. I told them both that I hoped that this had been an 'Excellent Adventure' for both of them, and I left the group to leave them together.

I sometimes wonder if they are still arguing with each other and naming people from the FBI.

I will end this chapter with the following image. It's a screenshot of a scammer pretending to be Keanu Reeves, calling himself 'kenue revess', telling another scammer from Nigeria who is also pretending to be Keanu Reeves to 'Stop proving that you are real'.

kenue revess

Stop proving that you are real

Seen by Keanu Reeves

I think I took the red pill.

## 'MY PEAS WILL STICK TO THE BOTTOM'

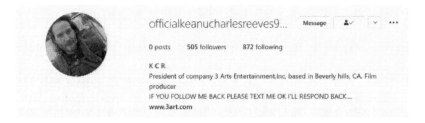

officialkeanucharlesreeves9...  Message  &#x2714;  &#x2304;  •••

0 posts    505 followers    872 following

K C R
President of company 3 Arts Entertainment.Inc, based in Beverly hills, CA. Film producer
IF YOU FOLLOW ME BACK PLEASE TEXT ME OK I'LL RESPOND BACK....
www.3art.com

Yes, dear reader. It's another Keanu Reeves. Another Keanu Reeves started following me on Instagram! Keanu bloody Reeves! You might be thinking to yourself, 'Erm James, I am not sure that is the real Keanu Reeves because you have already had a conversation with two other Keanu Reeves's about which one was the real Keanu Reeves'. Well, reader I know it's him because his username has the word 'Official' in the title.

hi greetings from Keanu reeves.
Thanks for following me back.
😊😊

Oh my god!! Keanu Reeves!!

Nice to meet you. It's nice to talk to you today.

It's a pleasure Keanu Reeves! It's a pleasure to meet you

I mean, I could not believe it! Keanu Charles Reeves was talking to little old me! When someone mentions that Keanu Reeves is one of the nicest guys, it is so true. He really does reach out to his fans. Even when you don't even follow him on Instagram. Even when you're not even that much of a fan of his. I mean, I loved Speed and the Bill and Ted's movies, but how many of us can say in all honesty they enjoyed Exposed, Interrogations Gone Wrong, Extreme Pursuit and The Private Lives of Pippa Lee? As much as a great guy Keanu was for reaching out to his (sort of) fans, he was also asking about the weather as well as a few other things.

> How's the weather there?How
> are you and I hope you are
> doing well with your work and
> health....

He cares to ask me how I am and how my health is. I replied and told Keanu that I was broadly healthy, except for a couple of verruca's on my neck, which I was going to cover up in the swimming pool by wearing the verruca tie[35].

Anyway, Keanu and I just clicked. He asked what the weather was like and if I was healthy and I asked what movie he was working on at the moment. He said he was in New York filming John Wick 4[36]. I was really looking forward to watching it.

> Amazing!!! Can't wait to watch
> that!

> Be patient ok

OK, chill out Keanu. A little bit niggly from Hollywood there. But to be fair – he's under a lot of pressure. He's one of the world's biggest actors, a celebrity always in the spotlight, and he's always popping up your Facebook feed with a photo of him on the subway with a caption underneath saying how much he donates to charity. It turns out that Keanu has more problems than you think as I got this message from him.

---

[35] Patent pending.
[36] 7.8 on IMDB.

> Honey I'm actually busy working
> on my PC right now but I can't
> access a file unless i upgrade my
> 10S and I really need it for
> presentation by Dawn tomorrow
> please baby can you help me
> get Google play card of about
> 100.00$, it's actually for an
> European site.

He's got a bloody presentation at dawn (I presume the time, not the name) and has to upgrade his computer to download a file... and of course needs a $100 Google Play card to access this file!

A Hollywood celebrity asking me to get him a Google Play card – it sounds like it could be the plot to The Private Lives of Pippa Lee. Regardless, Keanu and I went back and forth on how a Google Play card could help to improve his computer, when in reality updates are all free. We started taking about if we would ever meet in real life if I ever got to meet the actual Keanu Reeves in real life.

> Do you think we would ever go
> travelling together?

> If so, would it be an excellent
> adventure or a bogus journey?

I couldn't resist that one. But, as these things tend to do, the conversation kept going back to getting Keanu Reeves and the $100 Google Play Card[37]. This presentation must be pretty important. I wondered what the presentation was about. A new movie idea? A 100-page presentation on the regrets he had in making that recent Bill and Ted movie?

Keanu was insistent that I stop what I was doing right there and go to the shop and get this Google Play card for him. He was really insistent. It turns out he's not as nice as those Facebook posts suggest.

---

[37] Working title of this book.

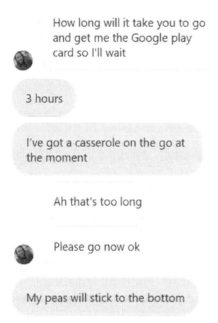

How long will it take you to go and get me the Google play card so I'll wait

3 hours

I've got a casserole on the go at the moment

Ah that's too long

Please go now ok

My peas will stick to the bottom

Imagine for a second messaging Keanu Reeves with the words 'My peas will stick to the bottom'. In a less star-studded world, imagine texting a Nigerian man pretending to be Keanu Reeves with the words 'My peas will stick to the bottom'. I just really like the phrase. My peas will stick to the bottom. I'm not even sure you can be putting peas in a casserole[38].

Keanu and I then started to talk about casseroles. Quite a lot about casseroles. I understood that Keanu had a very different lifestyle to mine. He was used to getting 'papped' all over the world, but it turned out after much pressing that he didn't actually know what a casserole was. I couldn't believe I was teaching Keanu Reeves about 1980's UK dishes. What's next? Explaining to Margot Robbie what a Fray Bentos pie is? Discussing Salt n' Shake crisps with Denzel Washington? I had thoughts of explaining to Denzil about the phenomenon that was Walkers Salt N' Shake crisps where you had to pour a small blue packet of salt over your crisps and then shake the salt around the bag. Despite this method, every single crisp would be devoid of flavour, until you got to your last crisp which would require 3 pints of water and a defibrillator on standby.

Anyway, it seemed that Keanu was starting to understand what a casserole is.

---

[38] Cassppperole. Turns out you can.

Actually I understand casserole
is a variety of a large, deep pan
or bowl used for cooking a
variety of dishes in the oven.

Not only did Keanu Reeves understand what a casserole is, he was telling me the meaning of what a casserole was, verbatim according to Wikipedia.

## Casserole

From Wikipedia, the free encyclopedia

*For the form of protest, see cacerolazo.*

A **casserole** (French: diminutive of *casse*, from Provençal *cassa* 'pan'[11]) is a variety of a large, deep pan or bowl used for cooking a variety of dishes in the oven; it is also a category of foods cooked in such a vessel. To distinguish the two uses, the pan can be called a "casserole dish" or "casserole pan", whereas the food is simply "a casserole". The same pan is often used both for cooking and for serving.

When I confronted Keanu that his explanation of a casserole matched the exact description of what Wikipedia, he started to get confrontational. He called me a swear word in a Nigerian language. I wondered if his next role was in a Nigerian drama, and he was just method acting. If he was, he was doing a heck of a job as the Yoruba words continued at me.

He then reverted back to his mother tongue and called me a fool in broken English. I replied as to why we were fighting over the definition of a casserole. Keanu seemed a bit confused and in a bit of a stew[39].

He then blocked me.

I hope you all go and see John Wick 4.

---

[39] I did have concerns about putting that joke in the work, but in the end, I decided it was stroganoff.

**INTERLUDE**

*Watch out for a scam phone call. The caller says "You have won £1 million or tickets to an Elvis Presley tribute concert. Just press 1 for the money or 2 for the show."*

Hopefully, the last few chapters have provided a bit of an insight into how Nigerian scammers operate and some of the lengths they go to try to get money out of you. On many occasions, when a scammer has finally had enough of me, I've been subjected to a number of Yoruba comments, insults and words. Here is a brief list of words, so you can learn a little bit of the Nigerian language, just in case you're ever in Lagos and feel the need to impress/offend the locals.

- **Alaye**: The term "Alaye" typically means area boy or thug in the Yoruba language but means something else here. In online chatrooms, professional scammers use the term to identify their colleagues in the business and quickly take on the next victim if they discover they're conversing with another scammer.
- **Ogun kill you:** Ogun is the warrior god of iron and war. He controls much of the material in the earth and represents primitive force and energy. In this instance, the scammer is telling me that Ogun will kill me.
- **Werey**: This is Yoruba pidgin street slang, 'Werey' in Yoruba means acting irrationally or crazy.
- **Onijare**: It's a curse in the Yoruba language that means "You will not reap the rewards of your labour".
- **Mumu**: The c-bomb of Yoruba. If you get called a 'mumu' by a Nigerian scammer, or a Nigerian in general, then chances are they are pretty angry with you. Although 'mumu' is also a loose Hawaiian dress, often brightly coloured, that hangs from the shoulder. So, if you are going to a Hawaiian themed fancy dress party in Nigeria and someone says 'mumu', it could be two things. Know your homonyms.
- **Oka Ti Fo/Ise Ti Ja**: This is a Yoruba word which means that a scam activity has been exposed.
- **Olorun je e ni iya baba aye, ko dara fun o ati iran re:** God is the mother of the father, the world is not good for you and your generation.
- **Your papa:** Fuck your father.
- **Your mama:** Fuck your mother.
- **Dey play:** You're wasting my time.
- **Ogun buy you a Breville:** As discussed, Ogum is the warrior god of iron and war. He controls much of the material in the earth and represents primitive force and energy. In this instance, the scammer is telling me that Ogun will buy me a new sandwich toaster. Ideally, the Breville Ultimate

Deep Fill VST082 Sandwich Toaster (Black). Sadly, no scammer has ever said this to me.

**LOVE AND ROMANCE**

Let's move on to the love and romance scam. Oh, love – surely the biggest scam of all time[40]. Love is the biggest scam that these crooks deal in and as sad as it sounds, they prey on lonely and vulnerable people. As discussed, they'll ask you a bunch of questions:

- What is your name?
- Where are you from?
- Are you married?
- Do you have any children?

Once they have this information (preferably that you are single, you don't have children, you have a steady income, and you own your own house) their aim is to gain their trust from you. To do this, they will create a persona of someone you can trust.

Usually, they will say they live in America. You can trust Americans, right? They'll tell you their job, which is normally a doctor. You can trust a doctor, right? Usually, they will tell you they're part of the military. Because, you can trust the military, right? If I had £1 for every new Instagram follower that told me they were a military doctor on a peacekeeping mission in Syria, I'd have about half a tank of petrol[41].

Scammers operating the love and romance scam will concoct a story about their life. They will also have a story as to why they are messaging you. In the case of 'finding love', usually they'll tell you they are recently single after their partner died in a car accident/yacht incident/cancer and that they are a single parent looking after their son/daughter. Yes, they will even use cancer as a tool to form their story. They want you to believe their story. They want you to believe that they are the only thing needed to form the perfect family. An example is shown below.

---

[40] Am I right, guys?!
[41] Satire

I'm married live with my children's but actually I lost my wife ,Mom, Dad with my two lovely brother died on there way going to london for an occassion,,,so since they had died things have been so hard and tough with me and thats why am really looking for the right woman who is gonna be there for me as a best friend and Lover...Infact i was just crying here now because its very painful to me, whenever i remember it.

Hang on though James, doesn't it take months and years to fall in love? I mean, we had 11 series and 2 X-Files movies, and still Mulder and Scully only just got it together! Surely, it takes time to fall in love?! Not in the world of scammers – time is money! The objective is to get you emotionally hooked quickly before you can escape.

They'll ask for photos of you and after a few back-and-forth messages, they can start the process to get you to be in a relationship with them. They'll tell you they are looking for their one true love, and they are here on Instagram to do so. I'm not sure why Instagram is the right platform for that to happen, but you just go with it...

They will ask about how long you've been single, if you have ever experienced online relationship before, what you look for in the perfect partner.

When the conversation is flowing, trust can be gained. Now they can look to exploit you for your money. This amount could be anything. They might tell you that all they want to do is to be with you – and for that to happen you need to loan them $500 for travel costs to come to your country. They might tell you that their phone needs updating, and if it's not, they won't be able to message you again. They'll tell you their father is in hospital, and they need $100 amount for his medical fees. In these instances, they will usually ask for money through CashApp, a mobile payment system that allows users to transfer money to one another using a mobile phone app. It's a quick and easy way to get money – perfect for scammers.

However, in other instances scammers will ask for much smaller denominations – as little as $20. In these instances, they don't want money. They want other collateral. This could be a steam card[42], an iTunes voucher or a Google Play voucher. By having a card like this, they can sell these on the streets, and get the cash they want. But, they will use whatever excuse there is to part with your money.

- *'I want to come over to you baby. But I have no gas in my car. Send me $20 and I will come and give you a good time'.*
- *'I don't have any food in the fridge, please help me eat. You wouldn't want me to starve to death, would you?'*
- *'I just need $50 to update their phone. If I can't use my phone, I cannot chat to you anymore baby'.*
- *'My bread maker is on the fritz[43]. Please give me a $50 iTunes voucher so I can get a sweet new Breville.'*

**Camera won't work if not Gift card is redeemed would be disabled in a few hours**

**Dismiss**

The scammer will persist with this. For many scammers this is how they get money. They'll use emotional language to convince you that you need to give them the money – *'If you loved me, you'd do it'*, *'if you don't do it, you must hate me'* and they'll be extremely persistent until they get their money.

According to the FBI, nearly 25,000 people reported romance scams in 2021, and their combined losses amounted to more than $956 million. This figure increased by 300% over the pandemic[44]. With restrictions on seeing people throughout 2020 and 2021, many people experienced feelings of loneliness and being isolated – which is a sadly the perfect fit for being scammed.

"There were widespread reports of loneliness, depression, substance abuse and alienation," says Monica Eaton, CEO of fraud-management company Chargebacks911. "So, it's no wonder that romance scams have been on the

---

[42] A steam card is a card that is used in the gaming world and used to buy console games.

[43] I'm absolutely in love with this turn of phrase.

[44] We're talking Covid, not the removal of Bounty bars from Celebration tubs.

uptick: If you're desperate enough, you're likely to overlook an awful lot of red flags."

Unless of course they are just pictures of red flags Monica. I can't stress this enough. Red flags are bad. Actual pictures of red flags are broadly fine.

So, let's look at some scammers trying to use love to get me to part with my money.

**HONEY TO THE BEE**

When a scammer messages you on Instagram, sometimes the best thing to do is to go on the front foot! Get them confused straight away. Remember, all these people want to do is build relationships with you and gain trust. So, if you show them that you have already had a relationship in the past – then so be it! The next scammer in this book is someone who called himself Eric. Eric and I have had an interesting history together. And by *'interesting'*, I mean *'a load of old bollocks'*. Eric reached out and said hello to me. I replied back.

> Hello Eric

> Is it you Eric? Eric from school? Did we go to school together?

> It's been 15 years since I last spoke to you!

'Eric' straight away, said it was him. What a wonderful coincidence this was! What are the chances? So eager to start a conversation, 'Eric' pretended that we were old school friends. As a result, we had a right good chat about the old days.

> I'm still in England. What about you?

> I am in Kyrgyzstan now working with my friends

Wow, Eric! Eric, who once went to school with me in England, is now working and living in Kyrgyzstan. Where is Kyrgyzstan, I hear you ask? Don't worry, I've done the research, so you don't have to. Kyrgyzstanis a landlocked country in Central Asia, bordered by Kazakhstan, Uzbekistan, Tajikistan and China. If there's one thing this book gives you, it's one truly excellent fact about Kyrgyzstan. Here is that fact.

If Scrabble allowed place names (they don't), Kyrgyzstan would be worth 30 points (along with Kazakhstan). Of all the one-word countries in the world, only Mozambique scores higher (34).

You're welcome.

Right, back to Eric. He wanted to know what had happened to me over the past 15 years. He asked if I was married. He asked why I was single. He asked if I had any children. He also asked what my occupation was. To be fair to Eric, these are classic questions that you would no doubt be asked at a school reunion as well as questions scammers love to ask.

Although we hadn't seen each other for a long time, it felt good to reconnect with Eric. Despite the fact he was living in Kyrgyzstan now, it was like the last 15 years were still a blur, and we were sat next to each other in Home Economics making sausage rolls. I remember one time in Geography, Eric, whilst we were all learning about cumulus clouds, Eric decided to act like a cloud. He was waving his arms about. It was so silly, so funny. But that was Eric[45]. Anyway, back to the 'real' story.

> Do you remember the last time we saw each other?

> No I can't

> We had sex!

> Replied to you
> > Do you not remember??

> I do

Now that Eric had remembered that we'd had made sweet love, I wanted to try to rekindle our love and see if we could get our relationship back on track. His reply confused me though.

---

[45] All bollocks.

Did you have a good time?

Here time in Kyrgyzstan is
2:21Am

However, it seemed that Eric also wanted to rekindle the relationship.

I can't wait to had sex with you
again

It seemed like destiny that we were to become lovers again. It was just the long-distance aspect of our relationship that we had to conquer. However, I had some news for Eric that I couldn't hide any longer.

Replied to you

Well I have some news for you

What

To tell you I was pregnant

It was only fair that I was open and honest with Eric. You see, we'd had sex in school and then he left quickly afterwards. It was then that I found out I was up the duff. Obviously, I had never spoken to Eric to tell him all this information, but now we had found each other on Instagram, I could tell him the wonderful news – that he was a father to a wonderful little girl.

This is your daughter

You are the father

Now, I realise that telling an old flame on Instagram that they have a 15-year-old daughter can be quite unsettling, and Eric was certainly confused.

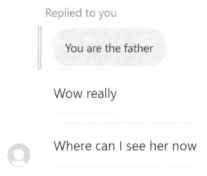

It wasn't as easy as this. You see, Eric was the one that left me all those years ago. He just popped out to get us both a Fray Bentos pie, and never returned. I was so angry with Eric for leaving me. So very angry. I had spent the last 15 years raising my daughter on my own, with no help from anyone. It had been hard. So hard. I was exhausted, and for Eric to suddenly want to be in mine and my daughter's life, I just couldn't accept it – at this stage.

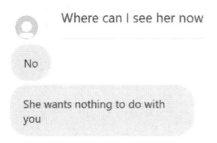

Where can I see her now

No

She wants nothing to do with you

I had to be honest with Eric and it was a weight lifted from my shoulders. I had finally told Eric that he was a father and I had to accept that he deserved to know the truth. As much as I wanted to keep him at arm's length, he had a right to know. I was suddenly struggling emotionally. Billie and I had a great mother/daughter relationship, and I had watched her grow up into a beautiful person, a promising singer who had the world at her feet. Billie was perfect to me. I trusted her. Billie had grown up to be a really mature, trustworthy person.

My conversations with Eric continued. He was flabbergasted when he heard the news about Billie.

Hun where is my daughter

Eric had some nerve. He knew where we lived. He had lived there too before he just got up and walked out on me! I couldn't afford to move in the preceding 15 years. I was still waiting for my bloody Fray Bentos pie! Have you ever waited 15 years for minced beef and onion? I was angry, and I took it out on Eric.

I am still at the same address, you've not been looking that hard you pig!

I told your parents

Betty and Mike

While Eric had spent the last 15 years running away from me and his daughter, I had always kept in touch in Eric's parents – Betty and Mike. Betty was like a mother to me. She treated me like the daughter she never had. After what that bastard had done to me, we had got even closer. Do remember if you are still reading at this point- all of this is complete bollocks. I am not the mother of popular 90's singer Billie Piper.

The problem with 'Eric' the scammer was that he had to continue with the lie. He was out of his depth – but he had to continue.

This is me telling your father

Yes, he does look a lot like Peter, the battenburg loving elderly gentlemen, from a previous chapter.

By now, 'Eric' was confused and wasn't sure how to proceed. Imagine having a fake profile, contacting a stranger for the purpose of gaining money from them, but that person says they went to school with you, tells you were in a relationship with them, has a child with you and then send you pictures of your father to you. Quite obviously 'Eric' was a little reluctant to continue. I, however, was more than happy for this charade to continue.

Me and Billie are going to the cinema tomorrow, and do you know why?

Because we want to
Because we want to

Eric wasn't quite finished.

> Honey am sorry please forgive
> me am sorry

> I really look for you my love

If he wasn't going to get the Billie Piper song references from the 1990's, then he sure wasn't going to get this one.

> You are a bad man and I am
> attracted to bad men... like
> honey to the bee.

But just like Bilie Piper in real life, men in my daughter Billie's life all turned out to be bad eggs. Yes, I am looking at you Laurence Fox. Eric demanded to see his fictional daughter, but I refused. Eric then threatened my life.

> If you don't bring my daughter
> back I give you 7 days you will
> die

> I see are stubborn right your
> stubborn will lead you to dead

> Am with your pictures as your
> names i give me 7 days to bring
> my daughter back or you will
> die

After threatening me and telling me I had a week before he would kill me, I did whatever a single mother would do. I protected my daughter from this sick bastard. There's no way that I wanted that man anywhere near my daughter.

There was no way that She Wants You[46] Eric.

'Eric' then blocked me. Which was a shame as I had a load of Doctor Who puns to hit him with.

---

[46] Third single from Billie's debut album. No, me neither.

## A WOLF IN SHEEP'S CLOTHING

Our next scammer went by the name of 'Arthur Jose'. Arthur Jose is a middle-aged man with a lovely grey beard and a gym fanatic. He likes to post pictures of him standing in front of a mirror at the gym. You know the kind of guy Arthur is. The kind of guy who weighs themselves completely naked on the scales in the gym changing room. I mean, how accurate do you need to record your weight? That's the kind of guy Arthur Jose is.

Anyway, Arthur started following my account for no reason and sent me a message and we got talking. Talking about the usual things. I asked him what his favourite raisins were (his are black) and how he likes his coffee (he likes his black). Sadly, he didn't ask me who my favourite Roger is[47].

Arthur said he didn't want to continue our conversation on Instagram but wanted to speak to me on WhatsApp. However, he didn't want to give me his number. He was incredibly insistent on this. I wonder why. I was happy to give Arthur my phone number as he seemed a straight up kind of guy. However, to be security conscious, I told Arthur I would give him my number. Just at one digit at a time.

Are you a clown

You behave like a clown

There is nothing wrong with adhering to security protocol, Arthur! After telling me that I was behaving like a clown, I told Arthur that I couldn't give him my WhatsApp number, because I had something very important to tell him first.

What happened

---

[47] Black.

I can't tell you

Although I couldn't tell Arthur my secret. I felt like I could talk to him about anything. Sometimes you just know, and I just knew it with Arthur. We exchanged a few more messages with each other and I finally found the courage to tell Arthur my secret.

Ok. I had sex with a dog

Well, more like a wolf

Like a wolf dog thing

There, I said it. Having shared this secret with Arthur, it felt like a great weight had been lifted from my shoulders. I knew that Arthur would be understanding mature and would respond in a mature manner. But with speaking to Arthur, I knew he would understand. Arthur was different. I knew he would be understanding to my secret.

What the fuck

 Eeewwww

Were you sex starving?

Maybe not. Although I do like he 'sort of' understood because I was 'sex starving'. You know how it goes. You've been single for a long time, you've not had any form of intimacy in a while, and therefore you turn to…. Sex with WolfDogs!

We've all been there. I shared some more details with Arthur about my experience with the dog/wolf hybrid.

> Part dog

> And it just howled a lot during it

> But it took an hour to complete

> We had Wolf eye contact

My messages with Arthur got weirder and weirder. Regardless of me admitting I'd had sex with sexy wolf dogs, Arthur said he was *'having feeling'* for me. Bless him. I told him I had to go away from Instagram as it was time to have sexy times with WolfDog™. Despite begging me to stop, I told him it was perfectly natural for a woman to have her desires fulfilled by a four-legged furry fuck friend.

 You are sick somehow

I messaged him back half an hour later with an update. An update that I don't think he was expecting.

> I think the wolf dog infected me

> With its juice

> I got covered

> I didn't sleep for a week

> And now I have fur on me

My body was changing, and I started transforming into becoming Mrs

WolfDog™, I wanted Arthur to be with me. Arthur himself was dealing with a hybrid of feelings too. Despite my body growing hair, me walking on all fours and eating my dinner out of a bin, Arthur had decided he loved me and wanted to spend the rest of his life with me.

I had to try and address Arthur's feelings for me as quite frankly there getting out of hand.

You love dog instead of me

It was true. I was attracted to my special furry friend, however maybe me and Arthur could work together. Despite the fact I was covered in fur, and was only attracted to WolfDogs™, I had a very special idea that could work for us to be together.

Would you wear a wolf mask when we have sex?

And howl too

It's your classic love story. Scammer pretends to be someone else. Messages stranger. Stranger says she has sex with wild beasts. Scammer says he doesn't mind that and still loves you. Stranger gets infected with wolf juice. Stranger begins transformation into wolf. Stranger asks if you are willing to wear a wolf mask. Scammer says he's slightly scared. Stranger asks if you will howl too. Scammer reiterates he is scared. Stranger says she can feel the hair on her body grow. Scammer sorts of backs off a bit. Stranger becomes feral with huge glowing yellow eyes and fangs. I'll be honest, I've seen worse synopsis on Amazon Prime movies.

I just wanted one thing from Arthur, and that was for him to howl for me.

Howl for me Arthur Jose, howl for me.

What happened next can't really be illustrated well in written form – but if there's ever an audio version of this book – it would include the following:

Just like that, I got a voice note of a Nigerian scammer howling to me like a wolf. Scammers will do anything in an attempt to extort money from you. They will even howl like a wolf.

Then they will tell you to fuck off.

Then they will block you.

Which was a shame really as I had instantly changed back to human form. Well, you know how the old mantra goes. I used to be a werewolf but I'm alright nooowwwwwwwwwwww.

**DO YOU HAVE 'RUNNING STOMACH'?**

This is Ellie. Look at her. Beautiful, Coquettish. Divine. A right bloody bird. Ellie messaged me out of the blue and we got off to a great start, and I knew that we would be friends (or maybe more) for some time to come. You can tell from our first interaction that we were really going to hit it off...

 What have you eaten

A massive sandwich

With an egg

Firstly, I love talking about food. One of my favourite questions is 'What is your ultimate seven item English breakfast?' It's the perfect first date question. Why not take a little break from reading and have a bit of a think? Send a SMS message on your giffgaff phone to a few friends and ask them the question too.

However, you should know there are a couple of rules around the question.

1)  Two sausages count as two items, three rashers of bacon count as three items – you get the idea.
2)  One bean does not equate to one item – you are of course allowed a portion of baked beans. I'm not an animal.
3)  You have unlimited tea and toast.

I asked a friend this question once and he instantly replied with 'Four sausages and three rashers of bacon.' I'll be surprised if he makes 50.

Anyway, I went for the classic 'a massive sandwich... with an egg' and wouldn't you know it...

I'm so surprised we ate the same food

Are you kidding me? What are the chances?[48] Two people eating a massive egg sandwich at the same time. In many ways, it's like two villages hosting two carnivals at the same time... it must be fête.[49]

Ellie started talking to me. She got to know me by asking the usual questions.

- Where do you live?
- What do you do for a living?
- Are you single?

I gave Ellie the relevant information and we were starting to hit it off really well. However, she was to hit me with some of her past that shook me to the core.

I'm a single mom

My husband died 2 years ago

I'm an hairstylist

That's horrible. Really awful. Just shocking. I mean, who would choose to be a hairstylist? Although did you know one of the great advantages of being a hairstylist is that although the salary might not be great, there's plenty of fringe benefits[50]. But fear not, you can always turn a negative into a positive.

---

[48] Slim. Very slim.
[49] I make no apologies for that.

At least you had nice hair at his funeral

I can imagine the comments at the funeral...

*'I'm so sorry for your loss. But OMG babe, look at those locks!'*

*'You look FAB-U-LOUS! French plaits? It's what he would have wanted'.*

*'They say the widow shouldn't bring a plus one to a funeral, but OMG, you brought your new bob, and I love it girl'.*

After that bombshell, our conversation turned to pretty normal stuff as we got to know each other, and we could feel ourselves getting closer and being more open and more honest with each other. The irony being of course that neither of us was in any way being honest. Ellie asked me what I was currently doing, and I replied with the fact I was reading my book.

I told Ellie I was reading a book called '50 Ways to Cure Your Hay Fever' which despite the title, hadn't worked at all and as a result, I'd sent the author a snotty email[51]. Anyway, Ellie and I were growing closer. I asked her what she likes to do in her spare time.

 I love playing snocker game

She likes to play snocker. Now, I know what you're thinking. That's just a small typo – she actually means snooker. So, I replied back with '147' – the maximum score in snooker, so that she could correct herself.

---

[50] I don't know what's happening to me.
[51] Zing.

Replied to you

147

What do you mean by 147

Nope. Nothing to do with snooker. It's snocker. Maybe a cross between snooker and soccer? Is snocker the game where there's six goals on a rectangle pitch and you use your cue to get the ball in the net? A bit like footgolf? Honestly, am I the only one with ideas?! This led me to thinking of which football ground would host a game of snocker? Of course, it had to be Jimmy White Hart Lane[52].

I was intrigued about what snocker was and how you played it. I was fascinated about how you get into playing snocker. Do you start playing snocker at school? Were we the only people who had heard of snocker? Why am I talking to a scammer about a made-up sport called snocker on a Sunday morning at 7am?! Honestly James, what are you doing with your life?[53] Anyway, I probed Ellie further and asked her love of snocker...

What is your favourite part of snocker?

I like standing at the left side

There you have it. 'Standing on the left side'. It made me want to run into JJB Sports and get as much snocker gear as possible. Although I didn't know anything about snocker, I wanted to impress Ellie with my snocker knowledge, so I sent her a message hoping to create some snocker frisson[54] between us.

---

[52] I admit I have a problem with very shit jokes in this chapter, but let's try and get through it together.

[53] That sentence is more for me than it is for you, dear reader.

[54] 'Snocker Frisson' once played the Pyramid stage at Glastonbury in 1994.

Replied to you

> Have you ever scored a D2R6
> during snocker?

 Yes of course

It seemed that Ellie was a very experienced snocker player. She once scored the much-coveted D2R6 trick special at Butlins in Minehead in 1991. Only a few people have done that in snocker history – Charlie Talc scored two famously in the World Snocker Championships of 2006 and Pete Scuffle-Shuffle scored one on his own in his basement. But it was never proven. And the cue he used was made from basmati rice.

I asked what Ellie's top score in snocker was (six), how often she played (twice a week) and when she started playing snocker (after her parents died in a car accident).

Now – that's enough snocker talk. Ellie and I were getting closer and closer. In fact, after a while (30 minutes) Ellie told me that she loved me and wanted to spend the rest of her life with me. This was great and I just knew that Ellie and I were going to be so happy together. There was only one issue. I was already in a relationship with someone called Lisa. I broke the news to Ellie that I couldn't be with her because of my relationship status. Although I had feelings for Ellie, I couldn't break things off with Lisa. I was in a love quandary.

> Just tell are that you are not
> interested in the relationship
> again

> Tell her you have seen a better
> love

 The right person for you

I had to make a choice. On one hand, there was Lisa. A reliable partner.

Someone who had a steady income, who worked hard to provide for their family. Someone who had seen me at my best and seen me at my worst. Someone, who although completely made up, was an absolute dreamboat – and who I wanted to spend the rest of my life with. On the other hand, there was Ellie. Ellie was someone who I had only known for 90 minutes, wasn't in any way real, and was a huge fan of a game called snocker that also didn't exist. I was in quite the relationship pickle. After a big mug of Mellow Birds, a couple of bourbons and some quiet contemplation, I made the difficult decision. I was going to end my relationship with Lisa, and I was going to try and give things a go with Ellie the scammer.

There was only one thing. I had to tell Lisa the news. I knew that this would break her heart. I told Ellie I was travelling over to Lisa's house to tell her that the relationship was over and that I was in love with another person.
Nothing could go wrong.

In fact, things got off to a pretty good start. Whilst I was at Lisa's house, I was secretly messaging Ella to keep her informed of the situation.

She's just made me a cup of tea

At this point, you might be expecting one of this author's many crap jokes. But you would be wrong reader, because you'll be pleased to know I refuse to do jokes about hot beverages that don't belong to me... That's not my cup of tea.

Anyway, I was having a cup of tea with Lisa, but then started to feel funny. I messaged Ellie straight away.

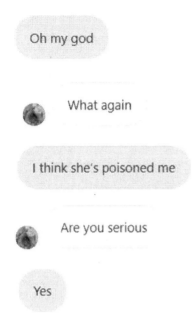

Oh my god

What again

I think she's poisoned me

Are you serious

Yes

I've been poisoned! There was poison in the tea! No! How could this happen? (Pretty easily, I'd made it all up in my head). But I had made a cardinal sin. I'd forgotten how jealous and vindictive my fictitious girlfriend Lisa can be! Lisa (fictional character) certainly didn't want me (playing a fictional character called Pippa Pegg) to be with Ellie (fictional character) playing snocker (fictional game).

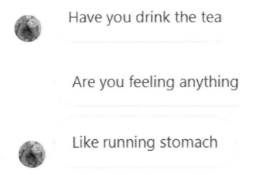

Have you drink the tea

Are you feeling anything

Like running stomach

I think we can all agree that 'Running Stomach' is a great name for an 80's death metal band. As the poison kicked in, all I could feel was myself getting weaker and weaker. Pain was surging throughout my body. I became hot. Then cold. Then hot again. Then cold. What next? Yes, that's right, hot. As I became weaker, my body was falling in an out of consciousness. I fell to the ground.

Desperately clinging to life, I could only think of one thing to do. I logged back into Instagram to tell Ellie what was happening.

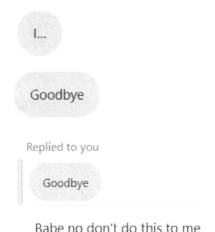

Babe no don't do this to me

Cue the Eastenders music! There was so many questions. Where will story go next? What has happened to me? Was Lisa a killer? Is there a murderer on the loose? What kind of tea was it? Why was the woman in the newsagents wearing mittens? Will the author make another crap joke in this chapter? There was 10 minutes of silence. I then messaged back.

Oh no... The bloody feds are involved. The fuzz. The narcs. The pigs. The po-po. The dibbles. The babylon. The rozzers. The filth. The bizzies, The five-o. The old bill. The porkchops. The double bubble. The blues and twos. The sweeney...And the police too. Police Constable Jeremy Kyle as well. Oh heck, what is going on?

> We have just found the body
> and this phone was next to the
> person deceased. Do you know
> the name of this person?

Ohh my god

I told him he should go to the
hospital

 Who poison him

Just a second Ellie, I think you have just made a classic mistake that wouldn't look out place in an episode of Quincy or Columbo. The po-po replied back to Ell-Ell.

> I didn't say he was poisoned.
> How do you know the deceased
> was poisoned?

He told me he's in is gf house

 That his gf gave him tea to drink

> It seems that you know more
> than you are telling me. I will
> send some police officers to
> your address to talk to you
> about this dead body

It looked like Ellie was in some serious trouble with the police. I felt at this point, the scammer would block me. The chances of scamming a 'dead' person were pretty low, and now getting messages from the UK police force too. It also felt like this story could turn into one of those six-part Netflix documentaries (that ideally should be just 3 parts[55]). Ellie, however, was either starting to get suspicious... or is a pretty sick individual.

 Can I see the dead boby

This is a police investigation. We cannot send photos of the deceased

I hope that Ellie meant to say 'body' there... and not 'booby'. Sending pictures of a dead person's boob is never a good idea. Trust me. So, it looked like the game was up for Ellie. The scammer behind Ellie's profile wasn't going to get any money out of me seeing as I was dead. I suppose there was only one thing to do, and that was to move on to the next potential victim. Or so I thought.

The scammer had other thoughts though. What would you do in this scenario? Cut your losses on move on? Not this scammer. Despite being in a situation where your potential victim had been killed, despite the fact you are being investigated by the police to understand if you have anything to do with the crime and despite the fact there was nowhere to go, Ellie Smith messaged Police Constable Jeremy Kyle with three questions.

where are you from??

what do you work

are you married or single

That's right, Ellie had had enough of me and was attempting to scam Police Constable Jeremy Kyle! It just goes to show that these people will do anything to try and get money out of you.

Then the scammer blocked me. Probably to play another game of snocker. Those D2R6's aren't going to score themselves.

---

[55] Yes, I'm looking at you 'The Cecil Hotel'

## DONGS OF PRAISE

This is John. I love John's bio. I really love it. It starts strong, doesn't it? *'Behold the fowls of the air'*. It also has the word 'barns' in it, which is great as I bloody love the word barns. If you delve into the quote from Matthew 6:18, it suggests that the definition of fowls in this context depends on which "fowls of the air" is used. Apparently, it can mean just natural birds, but it can also stand for demons, spirit of death, rumour spreaders, and messengers. All very intriguing from John. He seemed like an interesting kinda guy.

John sent me a direct message, and very quickly (message 3) asked me the following:

Are you married do you have children?

He then asking the same questions that scammers who use the love and romance scam. After going through the usual inquiries, it turns out that John is a doctor in Syria doing humanitarian work. He's a keeper! John and I got talking, properly talking, and we sort of fell in love. I know that sounds silly to say – but we had so much in common. He was a Doctor in Syria, and I told him my occupation too. I said I was a Saffron Decider, which he seemed to believe was a real occupation. We had a lot in common. I was a fictious person pretending to be someone else. And he was... well, you get the idea. The stars were really aligning for John and me. He was also a ruddy hopeless romantic.

Sometimes I wish there was no alarm clock because that is the only device which wakes me up while I am dreaming of you.

If you think about it – it makes very little sense. But the sentiment was that John is falling in love with me. Nothing could stop us from starting our life together. Not one thing. Nothing. Oh, hang on... maybe just one.

> Can you help to get amazon gift
> card let me update my private
> network please

Now, here was a curveball. John was asking me for money. I didn't want to be a Debbie Downer as I wanted John and I to work. I wanted John to overcome his short-term financial issues, so we could focus on our relationship together. But I needed to trust John. I needed to know that if I gave John some money, that he would return it. So, what would any sane person ask for in this instance?

> Please send me a picture of your
> neck

Surely John would understand.

> I will do that for you I promise
> you that please get me the card
> so I can have the access on my
> private network please

John understood. It was reassuring to see that in our relationship there was some back and forth when it came to trust issues. It made me believe that John and I could be together forever. Two souls apart, but together forever. John agreed it was important and agreed to send a picture of his neck to me.

John, mate! What you doing?! That's not your neck! That's a nude dude who has just got out of the shower! I told John in no uncertain terms that he very quickly needed to understand what a neck was. John and I were on different pages it would seem. However, again I explained to him that I wanted a picture of his neck. His neck. Only his neck[56]. Just his neck. John tried again.

John, mate! I want your neck...
not your dong!

I have give you Want you what

Maybe the language barrier is why we were having problems. John had been working in Syria for so long that maybe he had got confused with some of his English. In Syria, they speak Arabic, so I searched what the Arabic term for 'neck' was. Turns out, it's 'raqaba', which sounds nothing like 'shlong', 'dong', or 'heat-seeking moisture missile'. I couldn't really understand where the misunderstanding was coming from.

However, there was more news to come from our relationship. I had been waiting to tell him some news. But I didn't know how to approach it. Like, when is the ideal moment? I decided it was just after he sent me a pic of his giggle stick.

---

[56] Great name for a band.

I went to a doctor

I'm pregnant

You are pregnant for who I thought you said you are single?

John was stunned. Seriously stunned. My thoughts and hormones were all over the place, and I needed stability. I told John that I had slept with a stranger just a few weeks ago and we hadn't used protection. As a result, I was going to be left with a baby that I would have to raise[57] on my own.

Right there, I knew I needed John's support. John was a big part of my life, and I hoped that John would help me emotionally through this journey that I was about to begin. I kept asking John if he was happy for me. However, I could tell that 'John' knew the chances of getting any money out of me were getting slimmer and slimmer.

I offloaded to John about the thoughts I had about being a single mother. The financial pressure was weighing on mind. But it wasn't just the financial pressures, there was the emotional and my mental wellbeing and pressure of bringing this little bundle of joy into this world. I really let John know all of my thoughts and feelings. All of it. Fair play to John for acting in a mature manner.

Is a good new okay God said go into the work and multiple

I told John that regardless of the sex, I would name the baby 'John' after him. I told John that he was the most important factor in my life. I told John that although he wasn't the father, he would be taking a very important role in John Jnr's life.

---

[57] Rasi.

Even if it's a girl I will still call her
John

I will tell my child of you

John, I will need you to hold my
hand when I am giving birth

John seemed happy with this news. But like many love stories, John started blabbering on about bloody gift cards that I needed to buy him. I told John that I was too busy vomiting as part of my morning sickness to go to the store and get him an iTunes voucher. Despite this, John said some incredibly sweet things.

 And I'm not the one who give
you pregnant you have use this
your pregnancies to talk the way
you like

I told John that being pregnant was an emotional time for me at the moment.

I'm crying here John

My baby is crying too on the
inside of my body and I can feel
it's tears on the inside of my
body John.

I finally persisted and John that despite another human growing on the inside of my body, I would go to the store and buy a gift card for him. Just as I was getting my moccasins on, I felt some pain. I messaged John.

My waters have just broken

Owwwwwww the pain

Despite my waters breaking just 30 minutes after announcing my pregnancy, it seemed that John was not deterred by the timescales. It turns out that giving birth is a really painful experience[58], and I intended to tell John in no uncertain terms the pain that I was going through during my incredibly short gestation period.

I'm giving birth now

Despite John wanting me to buy a voucher for him whilst I was giving birth, we finally had a resolution. Well, I finally had a resolution. After a very painful three-minute labour, I was now the very proud mother of a beautiful baby boy.

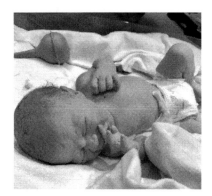

I was exhausted. It's not often you get pregnant and give birth within a 10-minute window. I was emotional. I was overcome with all sorts of thoughts and feelings. But I had my beautiful boy to focus on now. I knew that he was the most important thing in my life right now, and it was now my job to give him the absolute best life I possibly could.

Even John was impressed.

---

[58] More painful than hay fever apparently guys.

Wow you have a cute child

Thanks John. We had been through so much together in the 30 minutes we'd known each other. If I think to back when I first met John just half an hour ago, I wasn't even a mother. I was just a happy go lucky woman looking for Mr Right. I knew that I had a good friend in John.

Will you be the godfather?

 If you wish?

Thanks John. I knew I could count on John for support. He had been my rock since the father of my baby had disappeared into the night. I needed John.

John. As godfather of the baby I was going to ask you if you could financially help me out. Obviously I'm not working now so if you could pay for baby food and nappies for baby John, please help me out

I knew that I could count on John. John and I had been through a lot. We had a connection. We had something that most best friends don't have. We had loyalty. We had it all. I just knew, through thick and thin, that John would be there for me. Yeah, I was asking for some financial contributions, but as a single mother, I hoped that John that help a little towards the upkeep of my beautiful baby boy. As godfather, I hoped John would help us out.

 Fuck you

I'm sorry John? What? Have you dropped an acid? Have you drunk a pint of meow meow? Have you eaten an LSD pie?

John?

Someone has your phone

You wouldn't talk to me or baby
John like this

I knew John and the John I knew wouldn't be so callous. He was a good man. I tried to talk sense to him. I told him in no uncertain terms I needed help. It was time to forget his iTunes card and focus on the bigger things in life. I am sure John would help.

Send amount to baby johns
PayPal address

Babyjohnisnotreal@gmail.com

 Fuck you

They say that writing your life story can be very cathartic. It can also awaken some demons that you thought had been hidden. In this instance, as I write these words, tears fall down my cheek. John blocked me after this.

If you are wondering – what happened to baby John Jnr? Well, it's my book, and seeing as this story is a load of bollocks, I can sort of say what I like. John Jnr became the youngest operator on the Log Flume at Alton Towers. Too young in fact. It was discovered to be a human rights breach by Alton Towers letting minors operate the rides. They were heavily fined, and John Jnr never pressed that big green button again.

## A BIG RICK

What can I tell you about Alex? Well, let's start it off by saying, he's an absolute dreamboat! I mean, look into those eyes and try not to call the coastguard – because you could drown in them! Let's also talk about the eyebrows though. #hairy #traintracks #slugs

It also appears that Alex was interested in me too. I know, little old me. Fancy that! After the smallest of small talk, I mean the absolute smallest of small talk, he starts off with the old classic:

> Please are you married? Do you
> have kids and what's your
> occupation?

Well, after telling him what I do for a living, we were off to the races...

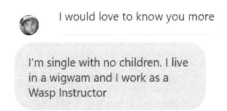

I would love to know you more

I'm single with no children. I live in a wigwam and I work as a Wasp Instructor

After knowing that I live in a wigwam, Alex was all over me. I mean, who wouldn't be? He wants some of that sweet tepee action. After just a few messages between Alex and I, things were already getting a little tents[59].

---

[59] Sorry, not sorry.

Can I get a picture of you here pretty 😊

Do you want a picture of my feet or shins?

Both

What a greedy man. Shins and feet! The greedy man. Well, I'm someone who doesn't like to put all out on a first date, so I just gave him some shin action and made him desire me even more.

And now the conversation took a slightly surreal turn.

Am taking a big Rick chatting with you here please

A big Rick. Where is he taking big Rick? To the park? To the dentist? Which Rick would this be too? I had to find out...

A big Rick? Who we talking? Parfitt? Waller? Certainly not Moranis?

I was hoping for Waller obviously. I miss Rick Waller. Fun fact, Rick Waller now works as an exam invigilator in Kent. Anyway, aside from Rik Waller chatter, Alex quickly turned the conversation to asking for a $500 iTunes gift card. I know right, what a shocker. After asking for a photo of shins in exchange for a $500 iTunes gift card, I turned the conversation into a quiz. Get 3 questions right, and you get the gift card! Everyone likes a quiz, right!?

Instead of the shin pictures, how about a quiz and if you get 3 easy questions right, I will send straight away.

## Question 1: What is 10+10?

I was pretty sure that Alex was going to get these questions right and earn himself a $500 iTunes gift card.

10+10?

Yes

I see you are joke

Not at all

20

Correct! You are 1/1! Well done.

Always start with an easy one. Although as Chris Tarrant used to say, 'They are only easy if you know them'.

> Question 2: What is 8x3?

> Ok

 24

> Correct! You are 2/2! Well done!
> Final question time...

Easy... This guy is no fool. He's 2 for 2! One question to go. Come on Alex – we're all rooting for you... OK – it's time for question 3.

> Question 3: Born in Bombay,
> India in 1952, this man is a Libra,
> and had his big break playing a
> character in the film The Bruce.
> He came to our screens though
> as the biggest and the baddest
> and since the show ended he
> can be seen snowboarding in his
> spare time as well as spending
> time with his son Dean...... For a
> $500 steam card.... - Who is he?

Yeah, it's a toughie isn't it! Born in India in 1952 and likes to snowboard in his spare time? Who is this mysterious man? At this point, Alex wasn't very forthcoming with his answer. He kept trying to make excuses. In the end, he gave up saying he didn't know the answer. It was a sad ending. Well, Alex no-one goes home empty handed. I said he could have a Pippa Pegg themed cheque book and pen, even though cheque books haven't been in use for about 20 years[60].

The correct answer was of course Wolf from Gladiators. Odd to think that at the time of writing, Wolf will be 70 years old. Wonder if Wolf could still climb that wall? A quick Google image search suggests he definitely could. The man is looking like a badass! I'd also forgotten that there was a Gladiators revival back

---

[60] Although my mate Steve still uses them.

in 2008 with Sky. Apparently, the format was updated to include water and fire. I think we can all agree that water and fire are crap names for gladiators.

Anyway, the scammer blocked me after this and merged back into the Shadow(s).

**ADD RALPH**

I'm gonna be honest, this one gets really weird, really quickly. I don't have much background on our scammer who calls himself 'Kelly', but the less you know about 'Kelly', the better. I will tell you now dear reader, this story gets pretty odd, pretty quickly.

We'll get to the story in just a second, but for the time being, I'd like you to put this book down and go and get yourself a large glass of wine. If you don't drink, then I want you to put this book down and get yourself a large glass of wine. If you have an allergic reaction to wine, I'd like you to put this book down and get yourself a large glass of red wine. You'll need it for later in this chapter. Straight out the gate, we're on to a winner here. It was a niche reply from me.

So what is your name and where are you from?

Settle down Cilla

Surprise Surprise! As we smashed right into a reference from 1993, Kelly gave me some information on who he was and what he did for a living.

My name is Major General Kelly Sungmin of the Korean Army, I come from Korea. I am a senior officer in the Korean army, currently in Syria (Damascus) on a peacekeeping mission.

It was quite a confusing scenario. The account had the profile picture of a female, the account was called 'Kelly' although they said that they were a man. Anyway, regardless, it seemed Major General Kelly Sungmin was a really good guy. However, I was concerned about Kelly. Being a senior officer in Syria meant he certainly had a dangerous job. I was worried about Kelly, and we were only just getting to know each other. Despite working in Syria (Damascus) Kelly told me about his personal life back home, and boy, he'd had it rough the last few years.

I lost my wife 2 years ago as a
result of blood cancer.
Ever since i lost my wife i'm
always working and have no
time for other things, she was
my first love and since she died
only focus on my job and have
no time for other things, it took
me time to heal

I was feeling sorry for Kelly. However, it wasn't all bad news.

But I have a daughter her name
is Rechel and she is 9 years old
now.

The Sungmin family certainly were pissing around when it comes to names. We had a guy called Kelly, we had a kid called Rechel, and we also had an attitude to women that Andrew Tate would probably approve of.

Most woman this days are not
faithful i mean the young ones
who don't know more about a
marriage life.

Although I didn't agree with Kelly's views on young women, I told him that I was faithful and would never stray.

I know. I am faithful. I am here for the long term. I have no eyes for the wandering dong.

I am really searching for a matured,God fearing,caring,trusted and honest lady who will be my wife and a mother to my daughter.

After Kelly had given me a very detailed description of the kind of person he wanted, I reciprocated and told him, in great detail, the kind of man that I was after.

And I'm after a immature, god liking. Uncaring, trustless and venomous man to be my husband...

Thanks for 'liking' the message, Kelly. Things escalated pretty quickly between us. Despite working as a very busy senior officer in the US army in Syria (Damascus), Kelly was always on Instagram. After a few more messages of getting to know each other, which probably lasted around 15 minutes, Kelly declared that he loved me.

 Yes I love you

Well, when in Rome (or Syria, Damascus).

I love you too

We were in love. Two strangers on other sides of the world who met by chance, and just fell in love. What are the chances? We had the rest of our lives to spend with each other. Together we were on a path of destiny together. You could tell the frisson between us.

I have told my daughter about you

That's lovely. I've told my local newsagent about you...

It was love! True love! Alas, it wasn't long before Kelly asked me for $1,500 to pay for a retirement letter. This letter would go to his boss in Syria (Damascus) and he would be granted indefinite leave of his duty. Kelly wanted to leave Syria (Damascus) to be with me and the only way that was going to happen was if I paid $1,500 for a retirement letter. Well, if Mohammad won't go to the mountain, the mountain must come to Mohammad. I announced that I would be going to Syria myself to meet Kelly for the first time!

Was he excited about this? Was he looking forward to this? Not really, no. He said Syria (Damascus) was a very dangerous place and then sent me photos of a dead soldier. An actual photo of an actual dead body. He then sent me another picture of a dead soldier. Then another. And another. Hey Kelly, stop sending me pictures of dead dudes, you ruddy lunatic!

Despite sending pictures of the recently deceased soldiers, our love could not be stopped. And to represent our love, Kelly sent me a picture of two wolves making a heart shape with their breath. It was one of the oddest photos I had ever seen, and I thought it wouldn't be out of place as cover art for a Kula Shaker album.

If you remember, I did say there was going to be part of this chapter where you need to have a glass of wine to hand. Now is the time to start drinking. I would also like to let you know there is some saucy chat coming up. If this book was a Guns N' Roses album, there would be one of those 'explicit lyrics' stickers on the cover. I'd say it gets up to a 7/10 on the sauce-o-meter. If you happy with a 7/10 on the sauce-o-meter, then read on.

Kelly told me he'd a dream about me, and then told me in great depth what that dream entailed.

> I woke up. Looking over to my right I see you fully naked, each breath bringing your lovely tits up and down.

> I looked down at my massive hard on and all the memories came flooding back like a tidal wave. Everything I just did, everything WE just did. It all seemed like a dream.

How's the wine? Got any absinthe to go with it? You might need it after the rest of this chapter. What you have just read is the mushroom vol au vent canapé, and you're just about to be served a family sized Pukka pie of pure filth. Take a large sip of wine now. Kelly continued on with more of his 'dream'.

> I reached down and grabbed one of your boobs and squeezed it softly. A light moan escaped your lips. You rolled over slightly and opened your legs a bit so I had a partial view of your pussy.

Yeah, we're big and deep into it now. (Oh heck, even I am getting in on the act now!) I like 'partial view' – like it's one of those restricted view seats you get in the theatre – where you save money on the ticket price, but you're left with a bad neck for the next three days.

Also, shout out to the time my wife and I went to a restaurant and ordered off the pre-theatre menu knowing full well we had no intentions of going to the theatre afterwards. Such naughty rascals.

Anyway, just in case you were thinking that was the end of the sauce, think again. It gets even saucier. This chapter should be sponsored by Dolmio. Put the kids to bed. Lock the door. Pray to the Lord. However, before Kelly provided anymore of his incredibly explicit dreams, I tried to cool things down by taking the conversation is a slightly different direction.

> Is the dog getting involved too?
> Tell me he does

 No honey

This part of the book will forever be known as the 'Wetherspoons Tagliatelle' — as it's pretty much 100% sauce. Make sure the door is locked, the kids have gone to bed and take a big gulp of your wine. If you're reading this on a public transport, it might be worth putting the book away. It's also not a great look to be having wine on public transport. To be honest though, if you are on public transport and feeling brave, why not start reading the book out loud? You'll probably get the seat to yourself. Or maybe the whole bus. After five minutes, you might actually be driving the thing.

 > I ran my fingers up and down your slit and slipped a finger into your Pussy. Another moan came out of your lips as I pushed the finger in and out.

Just like the author, I hope you have just downed a Corky's apple sour shot whilst having a cold shower to rid yourself free of the sexy chatter. If you have made it this far, congratulations. We're over the most of it now. Give yourself a couple of deeps breaths and let's all move on, shall we? Once again, I tried to change the subject.

If things were going to get sexual between Kelly and I, I think it only fair that we add my pet dog Ralph into the mix and make it a weird sexy canine-based threesome. I was adamant that my dog Ralph be part of our little adventure. Kelly seemed less invested.

Make no mistake, I was pushing for a threesome with my new Instagram friend and my dog at this point. I just thought that our relationship could only continue if we were to add my pooch[61] to it.

---

[61] Not a euphemism.

Add Ralph

 Ok

Say his name

I add Ralph to it

Now continue...

Yes! Ralph is in! It's me, Ralph the dog and Kelly. Now, I know I said we were over the saucy stuff. Well, there is just one more naughty message left. We are near the end though; I promise you reader. Imagine you are on the obstacle course on Gladiators; it really is just the travelator to go.

> You were really stretched out from what we did so I pushed in a second finger. The sound of my fingers going in and out was making me really horny, it was one of the best sounds I�ve ever heard, well there is one sound that�s better but I�ll get to that later.

OK, we're done. You can relax now. We are officially done. But I wasn't done with Kelly, who seemed hellbent on making this all about me and him, and not interested in Ralph the dog. Well, that's not what's happening here – I want Ralph involved.

Yeah but where is Ralph?

 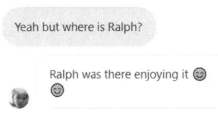 Ralph was there enjoying it 😊
😊

This wasn't good enough. I don't want Ralph just in the same room as we get up to some sexy time. I want him to be an active competitor. In some sort of weird furry threesome.

So, now we're in a situation where a Nigerian scammer is having to improvise a fictional sex situation with himself playing the role of a widow from USA with a woman (who is really a man with too much time on his hands) and a dog called Ralph that also doesn't exist.

Kelly and I went back and forth – him wanting to have some sort of dirty Insta chat – and me trying to shoehorn a fictional dog into proceedings to make things as awkward as possible. Here's an example of Kelly wanting to do InstaSex[62].

What does Ralph do to you?

Nothing Ralph happy that I am having sex with you 😊😊

---

[62] Is that what the cool kids are calling it?

And then there's me trying to add a fictional furry friend to proceedings...

Ralph wants you

Say it

Ok

To make thing a little more interesting, I decided to make Ralph a reality.

This is Ralph

Kelly replied with just one word.

Oh

I was trying my best to make things a bit awkward for Kelly. I mean, it was quite weird for me typing these messages, but at least I knew what was going on. This was a Nigerian scammer who was getting further and further away from any potential money and more and more involved sexually with me and an aggressive dachshund.

I said nothing why are you adding Ralph to it?

I want Ralph to touch you

Will you allow it?

You need to put your head in there

 I see you are not enjoying the sex dream

I want you to put your head in Ralph's mouth now

How

 I can't do that

Oh yes you can. I kept this going for a long time. Too long really. In the end Kelly blocked me.

I couldn't understand why to be honest. He was so close to getting that $1,500 retirement letter too.

**Green With Envy**

Irakibhassan  [Follow Back]  ...

41 posts     389 followers     7,160 following

rakib_hassan
HAPPY CHOICES: Applying the science of happiness and motivation to take control of
your success 🔵🔵

> MY name is Steven Donald from
> Santa Ana California USA my
> dear

This is Steven Donald. I think if my name was Steven Donald, and I could choose any username on Instagram, I would go with either 'Steven Donald', 'Steve Donald' or 'SteDon'. Steven Donald didn't go down this route though. This Steven Donald is a maverick and went with the username 'Irakibhassan'.

Anyhow, Steven messaged me out of the blue[63] and we were getting on swimmingly. He asked where I was from. Standard. He asked me what my occupation was. Standard. He asked me what my relationship status was. Standard. He asked me my age. Standard. He told me about his past in great detail even though I hadn't asked for it. Standard.

> In my own case, I'm a widower.
> My wife died of a leukemia
> cancer 7 years ago and I have
> just one son , name Kenny , he
> lives with his gardener in Santa
> Ana California USA and also
> school in a Borden school!

I felt bad for Steven's child Kenny. Not only had his mother died of an awful illness, not only was he called Kenny, but he was living with his gardener. You'd think it might be 'guardian' – but no, it seemed that Kenny was living with a horticulturist in California.

Steven told me his occupation. It was quite the coincidence that many of the scammers I spoke to always had the same role, in the same country, looking for

---

[63] Not green.

the same thing.

I'm an Orthopedic Surgeon
Doctor, I'm on a relief
assignment working with the
United Nation (UN) on a peace
keeping mission here in Yemen.
What is your profession?

What is your profession my dear

After telling him my profession (which he didn't query at all[64]) our #bantz
moved up another level. As explained, scammers will want to get you over to
another communication platform so they can protect their Instagram account
from being closed. Steven asked if I wouldn't mind continuing the conversation
on Google Hangouts. Sadly, I wasn't on Google Hangouts.

I'm not on hangouts. I'm on
Google JanitorFlush. You on
that?

As well as inventing any job occupation, you can also make up any social media
platform and a scammer will rarely question it. Many a time I have told a
scammer that I cannot chat to them on Telegram as I am not on it, but I am on
such platforms such as Sega DiscWazzock, ChatterSlapper, Cadbury Talk and
Mouth Brigade[65].

Steven then really wanted the conversation to continue on WhatsApp. Sadly,
for Steven, I wasn't on WhatsApp — and there was a really good reason for this.
Steven asked me why I couldn't download either WhatsApp or Google Chat.
What was the reason? Was it that I simply refused to give more details to
another giant corporation? Was it that I didn't want my data being shared to
third parties? Was it that I simply didn't have enough space on my phone? The
truth was a little different.

---

[64] I said my job title was 'Professional Cheryl Baker'.
[65] Working title for Sleeper's fourth album.

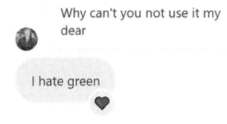

Why can't you not use it my
dear

I hate green
♥

Thankfully, Steven 'loved' my message, so it seemed he understand the
concerns I had. I simply cannot and refuse to download any app that is green.
Some people believe in God. Me? I refuse to have any apps on my phone that
are green in colour. If that's a criminal offence, lock me up!

Are you Downloading it my dear

It turns out Steven didn't really understand what I was saying. Maybe he
thought I wasn't being serious. I was being serious. I told Steven the reasoning
as to why I had this issue.

I had a husband once. His name
was Peter Green. He was
horrible. He was bloody awful.
As a result I cannot look at, or
even hear the word 'green'.

It's the same reason why Kim Kardashian threw away all her compasses when
she split up with Kanye. It's the same reason Angelina Jolie has never been to a
quarry since her breakup with Brad and it's the reason Katie Holmes now likes
to take her holidays on land since breaking up with Tom[66]. Try as I might,
Steven was desperate for me to download it.

---

[66] Kudos if you got all three of those.

Please just use it because of me
my dear please

Please my dear

 Just use it because of me please
my dear

As I have stated, scammers will do what they can to chat away from Instagram. WhatsApp is usually their least favourite alternative because it's their phone number they're giving out. However, in this scenario, scammers will always ask for your phone number to add on WhatsApp, giving you less chance of seeing/checking their international code.

Anyway, Steven seemed adamant I download some other apps. Almost desperate. Once again, he asked me to download WhatsApp to continue our conversation.

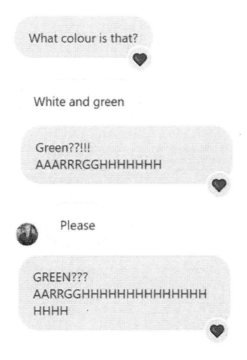

It seemed that Steven was confused (and a bit freaked out). The more he tried to get me to download WhatsApp and Google Chat, the more agitated I got. I'm not sure he truly understood.

Had Steven got the message? Did he understand what was going on? Did anyone really understand was going on? Was Steven going to persevere with this? Of course, he was.

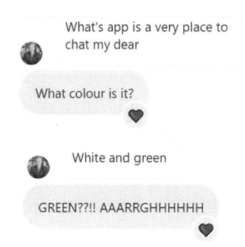

Slowly[67] but surely, Steven was starting to understand what was happening to him.

---

[67] Very slowly

There was a pause. Sixty seconds. It felt like a lifetime. No-one was messaging each other. There was a quiet serene state to our messages. A time where I think we were both reflecting. A time where we both planning our next move. A time where we both wondered if we were wasting our own time. I made the next move.

Was Steven starting to put the pieces together that I was just wasting his time? Was he slowly coming round to the fact that there was no chance of extorting money from me? Not really.

Yes why asking

Stop saying greeennnnn

 You ask me the colour of a frog

I know, but you know I hate green!

GREEN... ARRGHHHHHHHH

It seemed he didn't understand. However, he was getting angry. Really angry. He started calling me all sorts of names. Then he started calling me all sorts of names in Yoruba. He said that he didn't need money. He said he was rich. He said he didn't need anything from me. I didn't see this coming. I didn't realise I was talking to a very rich person. How did I feel about talking to a very rich man? I had to admit I was jealous of him. I was actually green with envy.

GREEN... ARRGHHHHHHHH

Then he blocked me.

**A MARRIK MADE IN HEAVEN...**

marrikbab     Message    👤✓    ∨    ...

10 posts     95 followers     2,640 following

**Marrik Babjuk**
I'm a urologist specialist, including general surgeon doctor

This is Marrik. Marrik is a doctor. He's a urologist specialist. This means he specialises in diseases of the urinary tract and the male reproductive system. Patients may be referred to Marrik if they need treatment for a condition relating to bladder, urethra, ureters, kidneys, and adrenal glands. Oh, and he's a general surgeon doctor too. He's your classic jack of all trades.

Marrik was also following 2,640 people – and surprise, surprise they were mainly women.

Despite being a urologist specialist (and general surgeon doctor), Marrik was asking me for $200 so he could buy a bicycle. You'd expect that his work might have a Cycle to Work Scheme, but alas that wasn't the case. When I explained to Marrik that I could not afford to send him $200, he came up with one of the best turns of phrase I have ever heard.

Are you pulling my hands? You are the one who ask of what i need now you turn me for a joke. I don't need that, just want to know whom you're. if you don't have money, ask me i can help you with money and stop that expensive joke.

I would never pull your hands. One of the last thing I would do is pull your hands. It's not fair to pull hands so I am not pulling your hands.

Marrik was quite persistent in me buying him an iTunes gift card – and so after some pleading, I finally gave in and got him one. I was pleased that he would use the iTunes voucher to buy himself a bicycle. Because that's what you can buy with an iTunes voucher in your local Our Price shop. *'Hey, can I get the new*

*Beyonce album, the latest EP from Arctic Monkeys. Oh, and an 18 gear Shimono Apollo bike as well.'*

I looked again at Marrik's profile photo. I couldn't resist the suited middle-aged man. So, I went ahead and purchased an iTunes card for him. It was what he wanted and to be fair to Marrik, he seemed over the moon with this. He asked me to send a photo of the receipt and the iTunes card. I advised the following:

> For security purposes I will send one number at a time. When I send the number please reply back with 'I understand what is happening. This is real. We're all real' and I will text the next number. If for any reason that message is not received I will assume you've been compromised and we must start from the beginning. I presume you understand.

> Snap it and send me copy of scratch card

Oh no – Marrik wasn't understanding the highly important security aspect of this transaction.

> That's the incorrect response. Please respond with the correct message.

> 4

> You are not correct

> That's the incorrect response. Please respond with the correct message.

> 4

This went for some time. Too long to be honest. Even I was getting a bit bored of copying and pasting the same message to Marrik. Marrik seemed to be a little confused which later dissipated to anger with every passing message. But rules be rules, so I continued with these very important security measures in place.

> That's the incorrect response.
> Please respond with the correct
> message.

> 4

By this point, Marrik was getting quite annoyed with me, and at one point questioned if I was a fool.

> You are not serious is like you're
> taken me for a fool. i think you
> need medication.

He's right though, I am a fool. But I am a fool with time on my hands. So, the ruse continued for some time.

> That's the incorrect response.
> Please respond with the correct
> message.

> 4

As much as Marrik and I were arguing around an iTunes card, you could tell there was some chemistry between us. We were meant for each other – and there is no more romantic way than to get engaged via a direct message on Instagram.

Will you marry me Marrik and then I will give you the gift card?

 Yes i will marry you

And so, on February 4, 2022, Marrik and I got engaged. Some people said it was too soon. Some people said it wouldn't last. Some people questioned our relationship. But, like I said to Marrik, they laughed at the idea of Katie Price and Dane Bowers once upon a time. But love will always have its naysayers. I had no doubt that Marrik and I would prove the doubters wrong. I loved Marrik, it was as simple as that. I told him so.

I will gobble your cock down like a homeless man eating a croissant outside a railway station

Marrik and I were in love! I spent most of that day wedding dress shopping and telling Marrik in (to much) detail about some of the dresses I was trying on and I was going to look so beautiful for him on our special day. I have to say Marrik was as excited as I was about our upcoming wedding.

 Our Honeymoon should be in the ocean. you will dive into to ocean

Just one problem with that Marrik.

> Yes Marrik it shall be in an ocean. Although I can't swim

 Really! oh that will be perfect

> Slightly sinister...

Note to self: Try not to be left alone with Marrik when close to water. Anyway, Marrik and I were talking about what each other were having dinner when Marrik made the revelation.

i go buy you fufu with banga soup

 you don chop dry garri befor

You OK Marrik? Everything alright? Have you sat on your phone? Or have you accidentally texted some Nigerian dialect that was supposed to be sent for someone else? What is banga soup I hear you asking? You probably paid about £10 for this book, so it should fall on me to do the work and not you. Banga soup is a soup made from palm fruit and it is common in the Ghanaian, Nigerian and Ivorian community. The soup is made from a palm cream or palm nut base. The palm cream is combined with flavourful, marinated meats, smoked dried fish, and aromatics to create a rich, deeply flavoured soup that can be eaten with starch, fufu, omotuo, banku, fonio, or rice. I've never seen it on Ready, Steady Cook.

Thanks, Marrik. It sounds delicious. There was only one reply from me...

> Fufu with banga soup. How do you know my pornhub searches?! [68]

It seemed our honeymoon period was over[69], and we had to both admit that

---

[68] Childish.

Marrik and I were having some relationship problems. I was busy fictitiously shopping for fictitious wedding dresses for our fictitious wedding, whereas Marrik was still going on about this ruddy iTunes card.

> you are really mad
>
> send me a diamond spoon

Send him a diamond spoon? Marrik, what the heck? It's true that Marrik and I were having our first 'tiff'. I'm sure we would get over it and it would make us a stronger couple. I truly believed that Marrik and I would be wedded. True love always conquers. Just then though, I received some bad news. I rushed to tell my true love, Marrik.

> Sad sad news
>
> It's my dog

> What happen to your dog, is it sick?

I explained that my dog had given birth to a puppy – and in a sad and slightly surreal twist of fate – the dog had devoured the young puppy. I was heartbroken. Marrik seemed concerned too.

---

[69] Twenty minutes.

Are your dogs a vimpire?

Can dogs eat other dogs?

I have never see where a dog
eat another dog

It was horrible. Legs being
ripped off. Teeth everywhere.
And blood. OMG, the blood.
And gristle.

I was looking to Marrik for advice. I had witnessed such a tragedy, that I needed Marrik for assurance and advice on what to do next. I was so lucky to have someone like Marrik in my life. Someone I could lean on for advice. Someone I classed as a friend. A best friend. Someone I knew that in all situations, would know what do and find the best solutions when life throws you a curveball. I looked to Marrik for his wise, mature and sensible advice in situations like this.

You have to sue your dog to
court

Yes, Marrik! I had to take the dog to court and sue him. Sue him for what? I wasn't sure yet. What charges could you bring against your dog in a court of law[70]. Marrik was right, I needed revenge – and the best way was to prosecute my canine in a court of law. Here in the UK, it can take years for trials to come to court – gathering evidence for the prosecution, assigning documentation, witness gathering, jury selection - however in this instance – it wasn't long (25 minutes later) before we had our day of reckoning.

---

[70] 'Great Dane'gerous driving, anyone?!

Today is the big court trial

Me v my dog

 Okay that's good

It was the big one. In the same way that the Wagatha Christie trail divided an entire country (well, 60 million people versus Rebekah Vardy) this trial also caught the nations interest[71]. However, just as the members of the dog jury were taking their place in the dog court, we were hit tragedy.

The dog died in court

Can you believe it?

 Was the dog die in high blood pressure?

Yes, Marrik. It was high blood pressure. And with that, Marrik realised he was losing a battle here. He called me a fool and blocked me. Marrik – wherever you are[72], I will always remember you.

---

[71] I refer the jury to the evidence labelled K9.
[72] Nigeria probs.

## THE TANDY WOMAN

This is Ruby, or ruby_ruby_123455 as she prefers herself to be called. Although Ruby has only posted 11 photos, she has amassed nearly 700 followers. There's one thing that you should know about Ruby – 'She does not snub – because she is new here'. That mantra made me question a lot about my life – and I eventually decided that this is what I want on my gravestone when I die.

*James Billington.*
*Born: April 20, 1979.*
*'He did not snub – but he is new here'.*

Ruby started following me, and as I #followedback (hashtags work great in an actual book BTW), I got a direct message from her. This was the second message I received from Ruby.

Baby I need too change my
underwear can you help me with
that

You might think that this is a bit forward, but please have a word with yourself. How many times have you had some problems putting on your underwear in the morning to the point where you have to message a stranger on social media to help you out? No? just me? Anyway, after a bit of back and forth, I thought I would turn things around and ask Ruby a question.

Can you lend me some money?

 Get the fuck out of here man

How rude! Despite this rocky start, Ruby and I had started getting on quite well. However, I was getting bored of her calling me 'dear' – I wanted to be called something else. Not Pippa, I wanted to be called something different.

143

Call me The Tandy Man

Growing up in Stafford in the 1990, I was obsessed with the electrical retailer Tandy. We had a Tandy store in the Sherdian Centre in Stafford, and it was the place to go for all your hi-fi-based needs.

Fun fact: Did you know that Tandy was bought by Woolworths in April 2001. Sadly, both Woolworths and Tandy are no longer on the high street. Although, I recently took a trip to Dusseldorf, where I was delighted to see a Woolworth on the high street[73]. Anyway, despite a slight setback, it looked like I had a new name and Ruby started calling me 'The Tandy Man'.

As our friendship blossomed, so did the frisson between us both. Sometimes, it was just suggested comments, sometimes it was an innuendo, sometimes it was flirtatious.

To be fair to Ruby, she kept up with the pretence of it all.

Replied to you

> What colour underwear will you wear for The Tandy Man?

 What colour did The Tandy man love

Despite Ruby and I becoming more flirtatious with each other, it wasn't long before she wanted to steer the conversation into an area where she was more familiar with – looking at a way as to how they could get money off me.

---

[73] I got myself some 'Pick und mix'.

Do you have cash app

The Tandy Man doesn't have
cash app. The Tandy Man uses
GlandDollar. Does The Tandy
Woman use GlandDollar?

No The Tandy Woman does not
use GlandDollar

Of all the silly things I have done in my life, this might be one of my favourites.
It's a simple sentence – but I have somehow managed to convince a Nigerian
scammer to call themselves 'The Tandy Woman' and tell me they don't use a
fictional mobile payment service known as 'GlandDollar'.

Despite the ridiculousness of what was transpiring, it was clear and there was
no doubt that the sexual tension between myself and Ruby was off the chart.
You can sort of tell that by the kind of conversations we were having.

You are wise

 Yes The Tandy woman is wise

But just when I thought that nothing can get in between our love, Ruby AKA
The Tandy Woman went ahead and ruined it all.

 I need you to send me the
money The Tandy man

Why would she ask for money? Could she be a scammer? Could The Tandy
Woman actually not be real? Could she just be contacting me just to get money
off me in nefarious ways? I had to find out. I had to get to the heart of the
matter. I asked her straight up.

Who are you?

 The Tandy woman

Good answer. She knew what she was doing. OK, it was going to take more than this to crack her. I needed either Rosemary Boxer from the thriller TV show Rosemary & Thyme, or Laura Thyme from the thriller TV show Rosemary & Thyme to help me crack the case. Alas I didn't have Rosemary and Thyme. I tried another question.

And what is your mother?

 The Tandy in-law

Kudos to Ruby, it was a heck of an answer. She was becoming difficult to crack. I had one more question to ask. Could she pass the test? Or would she fail at the final hurdle?

And what is my grandmother?

 The Tandy grandmother

It was obvious that me (The Tandy Man) and Ruby (The Tandy Woman) were in love, and despite the fact, The Tandy Woman kept insisting I buy her a steam card, it seemed there was no stopping us as we continued on our way to Love City. Despite our love blossoming, I was busy with my family (The Tandy's) and explained that I couldn't really message due to family commitments.

The Tandy Man is here

But The Tandy Mother is here too

I am cooking for The Tandy Mother and The Tandy Mother's New Boyfriend

 Okay can The Tandy man send The Tandy woman the card??

I explained to Ruby that I was busy cooking for my mother and her partner. I couldn't just go to the store and get Ruby a steam card – it would be rude – and I didn't want to overcook my lasagne.

 So when will The Tandy man send The Tandy woman her card

When The Tandy Mother has gone

Can't The Tandy man just take just 2 minutes out of his time to send The Tandy woman her card

Settle your beak, Ruby! I am busy! I have to say at this point, The Tandy Woman was getting a little full-on. Chill your boots, sweetheart. I was getting it in the neck from Ruby, but I was very excited to tell my mother (Mrs Tandy) that Ruby (The Tandy Woman) and I were in a relationship (The Tandy's). I know... totes huge news! However, I was getting slightly annoyed at Ruby's insistence I buy her a steam card.

> The Tandy Mother is very demanding

> I will however tell The Tandy Mother that The Tandy Man has fallen in love with The Tandy Woman

But, just like that – bad news was around the corner. I was just about to tell my mother and her partner the great news – that her baby boy was dating a woman from Instagram – when all of a sudden, bad news happened!

> Oh no

> Something bad has happened

 What happened to The Tandy man

> I told The Tandy Mother about us

I had a feeling that something bad had happened. I had that feeling because I was controlling the narrative.

> The Tandy Mother was really happy

> But The Tandy Mother's New Boyfriend was really angry

> He yelled and kicked my dog Tandy Murray

Oh no! How dare he! Poor Tandy Murray! Why would he do this? What a bloody monster! How could he do such a thing? Why would he take his anger out on an innocent animal? Why was he so angry all the time? Ruby however, had some wonderful advice going forward.

 Tell him you love The Tandy woman the way he loves The Tandy mother

Sadly, it was going to get worse for me. Ruby asked how I was, and I had to be honest with her. Although we had only known each other a few hours, we had been through a lot. Because of this, we had grown a serious and deep bond based on honesty. I was in a situation where I knew I had to be honest with Ruby. So, I was.

 Hi how is The Tandy man now

It's been an awful night. The Tandy Man hit The Tandy Mother's new boyfriend after The Tandy Mother's new boyfriend kicked The Tandy Man's dog, Tandy Murray.

The police got called and The Tandy Man got arrested.

Obviously, The Tandy Woman was concerned about me and what charges the police were going to charge me with. You could tell how concerned she was because she asked to get her a steam card after I was released from the police station. If that's not true love, then Al-Qaeda has won. After more back and forth that involved the word 'Tandy' being used more times in a day since a Tandy strategy away day in Telford in 1998, we finally had a serious talk about our relationship.

So The Tandy man want to leave
The Tandy woman?

The Tandy Man wants to be with
you, The Tandy Woman and take
my dog, Tandy Murray with me.
Maybe also my cat, Tandy
Warhol too.

Enough of the Tandy chatter. I had some business to take care of. You see, I hadn't told Ruby that I was actually already in a relationship with someone else. I was torn. I was torn emotionally. On one hand, I had a real partner. A partner that existed in real life. But then I had a relationship with a Nigerian scammer on Instagram. It was quite the pickle I was in[74]. After much soul searching, I decided I wanted to be with The Tandy Woman. This meant, I had to break it off with my current partner. I explained all this to Ruby.

I don't like when The Tandy man
share himself with another
woman

Ok I will call the other woman
and tell her that The Tandy Man
is taken by The Tandy Woman

I told The Tandy Woman that The Tandy Man was travelling to his partners house with the sole intention of breaking off the relationship[75]. Nothing could go wrong. Or so I thought. Although Ruby insisted that I get her an iTunes card on the way, I advised I would get it after I had broken up with my current beau. Much to her chagrin.

I was texting Ruby as I approached the front door. I was nervous. I told Ruby that my partner had a bit of a temper and can be quite jealous, so I just wanted to make sure I did the right thing and that she took the news as well as possible. As I entered the house, I had a seat on the sofa. I got my phone out

---

[74] 'Quite The Pickle' – great name for a band.
[75] Never in the history of language has that sentence ever been written.

and sent Ruby a message.

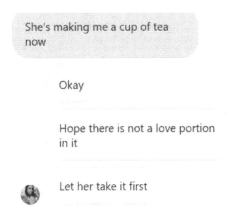

Oh my! Not again! I hadn't thought of this. She could have put anything in there. Why didn't I think of that? My head was spinning. My heart was racing. Had she done me wrong? Something was wrong. I text The Tandy Woman.

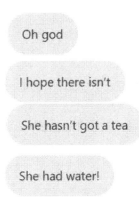

Clearly there was a problem here. After trying to end things to continue my relationship with The Tandy Woman, my girlfriend had poisoned me and was going to leave me for dead! I got my phone out. My eyes were blurry. I managed to get to Instagram and saw a message from The Tandy Woman. She knew it. I knew it. I may never get to see The Tandy Woman again.

Replied to you

> She had water!

Ohh no

I managed to put some words together to send to The Tandy Woman. I asked her to send help. I said I was in her basement. I told her I was drifting in an out of consciousness and I told The Tandy Woman that I loved her.

 Are you kidding

No, I wasn't kidding The Tandy Woman! I wasn't sure where my next breath was coming from. I didn't know what to do next. My breaths became shorter. My eyes started to close. I saw a bright light. Was this the end? I looked towards the light. Turns out it was the light of my phone screen showing me I had another Instagram message from The Tandy Woman.

Send me her location

 I have too get the police right over there

Thank God for The Tandy Woman. As I lay in my ex-girlfriend's basement, drifting in an out of consciousness after being poisoned, The Tandy Woman was here to save me. She asked me to text her the address of where I was. I typed any old bollocks address. It's amazing she didn't pick up on anything.

23 Swindler Avenue
Crook City
Scamshire
England
SC4 MMR

I'd expected the scammer to pick up on the fact I had been wasting their time. It turned I was giving them too much credit. The ruse continued. It looked like things were going to be OK. The police were being called and both them and The Tandy Woman would be here soon. Or so I thought.

On my way too the address you
sent me

I was called the my grandpa has
an accident

He fell down from the stairs and
he was injured

Oh no! The Tandy Woman's grandpa had taken a fall and was injured. She must be devastated. First, her boyfriend and soon to be lover gets kidnapped and poisoned and then her grandfather takes an unexpected tumble down the apples and pears. She also sent me a picture of her grandfather after the fall. Quite why someone would see an old man at the foot of the stairs, clearly in distress and their first action is to take a photo is anyone's guess. But I am not one to judge.

It does look like a pretty hard floor too. This did mean that The Tandy Woman's priorities changed, and she had to look after her grandfather. I was left drugged and hoped the police would show up soon.

Pretty soon after, The Tandy Woman started asking for another iTunes card to help pay for the hospital fees because of her grandfather's fall. Say what you want about the NHS, but at least you don't have to pay for all your healthcare needs with an iTunes card. After miraculously recovering from my poisoning in record time, I made the effort to ask on the health update of The Tandy Woman's grandfather. Despite asking consistently for an iTunes card for hospital fees, I told The Tandy Woman I had something even better for her! I said to help cheer up the old timer, I had written a poem for him, and I had no doubt this would be the catalyst needed to get him up on his feet in no time.

# Grandad Tandy In Law

He fell, he fell
Is Grandad OK?
He fell, he fell
He is elderly.

He fell, he fell
Who pushed him? The Tandy Nan?
He fell, he fell
It wasn't The Tandy Man

He fell, he fell
He hit his knee hard
He fell, he fell
Who wants a Steam Card?

It seemed that The Tandy Woman didn't really appreciate the poem, which I was hoping to get a Pulitzer Prize, but it seems everyone is a critic these days.

It a very nice poem but do you
think The Tandy grandpa need
the card for nothing sake

The Tandy grandpa was telling
me not too tell you that you
might think we just want too
collect money from you that you
might not trust us

The Tandy Grandpa was very wise, and at least was fully compos mentis[76]. I finally agreed to get the iTunes card to pay for the old dude's medical bills. I

---

[76] I thought he was third party, fire and theft.

said I was rushing to go to 'my local store' to get the card. But would you believe it? They say bad things happens in threes and here was the third! Just as I about to leave the house I heard a thud from behind me. I turned. My eyes fixed on what I saw.

OH MY GOD

 What the matter

I couldn't believe what I saw, so I reached for my phone and instantly took a photo of the scene in front of me.

The Tandy Man's grandmother has had a fall! OMG!

 What all this

It turns out this was one step to far with Ruby. To be fair, it was one step too far for The Tandy Man's grandmother too, which is why she's lying at the bottom of the stairs at the moment. She called me a rude word in Nigerian and then blocked me. I hope her grandfather is OK.

It might be time to install that stair lift.

## FOOD FOR THOUGHT

This is Linda!

When I put this picture into the book, alt text automatically called it 'A woman with long blonde hair'. Personally, I would describe this as 'A woman with long blonde hair with her Bristols out on display'. Anyway, this is Linda. On her third message to me, she asked me if I would marry her. Third message! That must be a world record[77]! I didn't know anything about her – what her seven-item breakfast order is, if she has any allergies, her education, her job, where she lives – just boom! Straight in with a proposal of marriage.

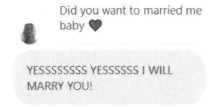

Did you want to married me baby ♥

YESSSSSSSS YESSSSSS I WILL MARRY YOU!

I couldn't believe it! I was to be betrothed to 'a woman with long blonde hair'. Wait 'til I tell my mum about this. And my actual wife. What will she say about this? I was so happy; I was in dreamland. And not the actual Dream Land – the store that sells beds at discounted prices on the outskirts of Cannock. I was the happiest I had ever been. Engaged! Nothing can go wrong. Nothing! Not one

---

[77] Rupert Murdoch might have something to say about that.

thing. Nothing. Like I said, nothing! I couldn't wait for my next message from Linda. Could it be about where we spend the rest of lives? Could it be where we would honeymoon? Could it be about if we would homeschool our children? I wondered what it could possibly be.

> I need some money to buy food in my home I don't have any money to buy food please can you do it for me baby 🖤

Oh.

Surely, she wasn't after my money? Surely our relationship, despite brief so far, was one for life. I can imagine our little blonde-haired children running in the garden. I can see our two dogs dry humping grandpa who'd had another fall. I see many things. Not all of them pertinent to this narrative if I'm honest. I thought to myself that if Linda was struggling financially, then surely it was only right that her partner for life helps out. But first I needed to make sure she was telling me the truth.

> Send a picture of your fridge

I just wanted to make sure that she was telling the truth. If I am honest, I'd had a couple of people on Instagram telling me a few pork pies, so I was a little bit resistant to her claims that she didn't have any food in the house. Although if she did have pork pies in her fridge, that would also be a lie.

So, I asked Linda for a picture of her fridge. Fridge picture incoming...

What Linda has done here is confused the word 'fridge' with the words 'impressive photo of her rack'. Although, to be fair she is showing off her Zanussi's[78] in spectacular fashion.

You'd think you would have the foresight to head to google, type in 'empty fridge', click images and send that picture over to me. Sadly, for the scammer posing as Linda – it wasn't that easy.

---

[78] There's no way 'Zanussi' can become a term for breasts, is there?!?

Baby they have pick my fridge
from me I tell them too reload
the gas for me and have not
returned it back

trying to understand me baby
💚💚

If anyone can decipher this into English, you're a better person than me. We don't know who 'they' are. The government? The Tories? The illuminati? They've taken her bloody fridge though. I tried again to decipher the sentence. Linda has asked them to return the fridge with gas in, but at this point, they haven't returned it. Is that right? Anyway, I messaged back.

Please show me your empty
cupboards

You might not have a fridge Linda, but there's every chance you have a box full of Fray Bentos pies in your cupboards. I just wanted to make sure that Linda was telling the truth, and she didn't have a cupboard full of puff pastry pleasures.

They say a picture says a thousand words. That's good news for me, as my publisher said I was a few words short on this book. Back to the picture though…. We must talk about the wallpaper. What year do you think? 1989? 1979? I'd also be quite reticent to drink that orange juice even if I'd just returned from a two-week trek across the Saraha desert. To be fair, that kitchen looks like a crime scene. If the alt text for this scammer said, 'A woman with long blonde hair', then the alt text for this kitchen would read 'Has Fred and Rose West's fingerprints all over it'. It's fair to say I had a lot of questions to ask Linda.

Can I ask a question

You know how you said you need money for food

And you sent me a picture of your empty cupboards proving you have no food in the house?

However, why is it when you Google image search 'empty cupboards' if comes up with your exact image?

hotcore.info

Empty Kitchen Cupboard

Visit

To be fair to Linda, she was willing to keep the facade going for a little while longer.

> Why is it the same photo?

> Those repair use too put it
> online after finished done it

Those bloody fridge repair men! Gone are the days when a fridge repair man would come to your house, take your fridge away to be repaired, and return it in working order. Now they are taking a fridge away, taking photos of your empty cupboards, uploading the photos to the internet for no reason, and still not returning your fridge.

After a bit of back and forth with Linda and her fridge-based antics, she hit me with this.

> Okay, so the picture you sent
> me is not your cupboard?

> Yeah I can't lie for you am
> Just pulling your leg

> I want to know your reaction

What a wonderful practical joke? Take that Impractical Jokers. I can't believe I fell for the old 'I am pretending to have empty cupboards' joke! Anyway, it seemed that Linda had enough of playing around.

Zazuu sure

Zazuu sheer

Ogun kill you

If you don't show your
appearance

If you don't want me to kill you
show yourself on video call

After asking Linda how 'she' would kill me, I was met with the best response.

Am just pulling your leg

Linda really was the new Jeremy Beadle. Look out for 'You've Been Linda'd' on Channel 5 in the summer. Sadly, Linda blocked me after this death threat. I still sleep with one eye open. Not because of the death threat from Linda. It's more to do with the fact I'm terrified someone will take my fridge from my house and post pictures of it on the internet.

## #GERMANBYBLOOD

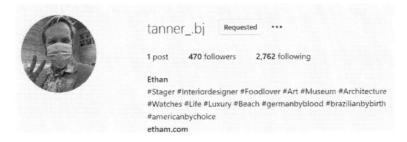

tanner_.bj   Requested   •••

1 post       470 followers       2,762 following

Ethan
#Stager #Interiordesigner #Foodlover #Art #Museum #Architecture
#Watches #Life #Luxury #Beach #germanbyblood #brazilianbybirth
#americanbychoice
etham.com

This is Ethan. There's a lot of hashtags that come along with Ethan. Those last three are simply #incredible aren't they! #GermanByBlood #BrazilianByBirth and #AmericanByChoice. Obviously, I'm sure he gets a lot of traffic to his Instagram account with people searching the hashtag #GermanByBlood. I do also love the hashtag #watches.

Do that mean he's interested and collects timepieces? Or he simply… watches. Two very different things. I passed a shop the other day that said, 'Watch Repairs Here'. So, I did. For an hour. It wasn't that exciting. Ethan also has a website etham.com – which is now up for domain purchase, so if you fancy it – get involved!

Ethan started off the conversation.

 I guess you're married

It's quite a bold statement to start a conversation with a stranger. 'I guess you're married'. Try doing that the next time you're sat next to a stranger on a bus – or if you are passing them on the street. I guarantee as soon as more seats become available – that person is moving seats. However, if they don't, they are a keeper. And that's what I was – I wanted to be Ethan's keeper.

I'm single

I live with my cat

Do you want my cat?

Yes

I want your cat

And, just like that – after five messages between us – I had sold my cat to Ethan. That's how you do business on Instagram. Short and to the point.

Now – fun fact – this is in real life, my actual cat. This is Missy! Couple of things you need to know about Missy. She's 20 years old and is an absolute legend to photograph. She also dribbles a lot (see photo) and has had to have a 'lion cut' because she's really old and can't really clean herself anymore[79].

Anyway, despite being 20 years old and pretty frail, I had sold Missy to Ethan on Instagram, and I wasn't about to go back on my word. Ethan told me he lived in the USA (#AmericanByChoice) and so, I was going to ship the feisty frail

---

[79] Missy has since died. 20 years old. Lived the life of an absolute queen. Full of sass. She also bit the vet on the way out too. What a legend. RIP Missy.

feline over to the States.

However, Ethan started to be a bit coy. I was trying to get his address so I could send the cat to him – however he was being very unspecific in where he lived. Why was this? GDPR? Had he not paid his TV licence? Was he a bad Vinted seller?

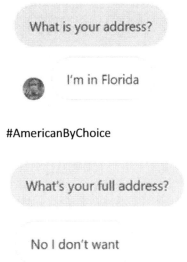

#AmericanByChoice

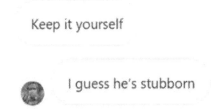

You don't want? Ethan? What is this? The cat is all ready to go! All packed and ready to be sent.

Well, Ethan - I would rather be stubborn than change my mind all the time. I was quickly finding out that Ethan was #AmericanByChoice but also #IndicisiveAndQuiteAnnoying.

Interest in the sale of the cat was obviously dwindling, however there was one thing that was quickly escalating – and that the relationship status between Ethan and myself. I know, who saw that coming?

Have you ever been in a relationship

Have I ever been in a relationship Ethan? Er, just a bit mate. But I had to play it cool.

Once

He died

He was pushed down the stairs

Yeah, a sad sad part of the story. but we do have a lovely little joke coming up. Read on.

For how long now

It only lasted about 3 seconds. Bump. Bump. Dead.

Ethan to give him credit, was undeterred. Despite me instantly selling my cat to him, and despite me admitting to pushing my former lover down the stairs, Ethan didn't seem to care about any of this - #AmericanByChoice #ScammerByProfession.

Ethan then sent me a picture of him and his daughter having a lovely time drinking some Aperol Spritz.

Looking like slightly disturbed Phil Tufnell, there was Ethan showing me that he was just an ordinary guy enjoying an Aperol Spritz with his daughter in an attempt to gain trust and lull me into a relationship that is faker that the photo you see. But hang on... Wait, just one second... Look more closely at the photo. Was it really Aperol Spritz that was being drunk by Ethan and his daughter? Is it? Could it be?! think it might be. I had to ask him. I had to approach the elephant in the room...

> Are you drinking blood?

I was concerned. Far from being the go-to drink my friend Tom drinks when on holiday in the sunshine, I was I'm sure we were all thinking it. Let's see what Ethan says to this!

 No I'm not

> You are!

> I'm calling the police

> You're drinking animal blood

I had to confront him. I had to confront Ethan and his weird daughter for drinking animal blood looking happy together like it's the most normal thing in the world. #AmericanByChoice #AnimalBloodDrinkerAtNight.

 That's not horse blood

Stop lying

You're drinking horse blood from a glass that looks like it's solidified sheep stomach

Why would you do this?

Drinking horse blood from a glass that resembles a sheep's stomach? Who was this sicko? Who was the real Ethan? Why was he drinking horse blood with his daughter? Despite pleading his innocence, it was obvious to me that him drinking horse blood was making him not fully compos mentis.

You are hallucinating because of the horse blood

Make yourself vomit and say the word 'Ginger' into the mirror 5 times

Break the spell

Ethan was off his tits. There was no hope for him and his daughter. Addicted to drinking horse blood. It can make you say all sorts of things.

Show me ur naked pics

When last do you have sex

Ethan was horny on horse blood! What a time to be alive. And here's me trying to give him a cat about 45 minutes ago. What would have done to poor Missy?

And I will drink your blood

It was at this point where Ethan sent me the best photo I have ever seen. It's nothing out of the ordinary – just a picture of a man holding a cookie. As simple man. A simple cookie. But the smile, the look into the camera, everything about this photo makes me smile/a little creeped out.

He said he was eating a cookie. I told him it wasn't a cookie, but was in fact, horse brain. I questioned Ethan why he was eating horse brains. And he blocked me. It's a shame. I hope Ethan is well. #AmericanByChoice #BlockedByAScammer #PhilTufnellsStuntDouble.

## JOBS – PART 1

One of the great constants in life is death, taxes and a scammer asking you what your job is. They want to know that you have an steady income, and you have money that they can try and con you out of.

However, it quickly became apparent that scammers don't really understand (or care) what you do for a living – so I realised I could write any old bollocks and get away with it. Here's a selection of some of my favourite 'jobs' I have had...

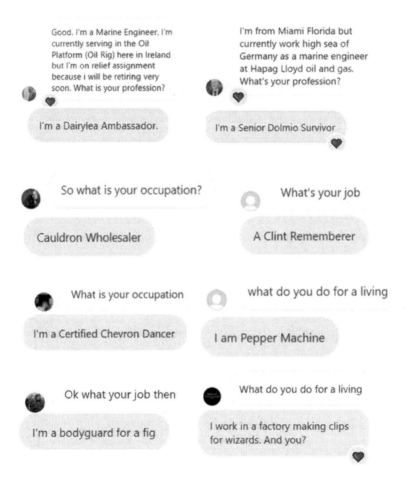

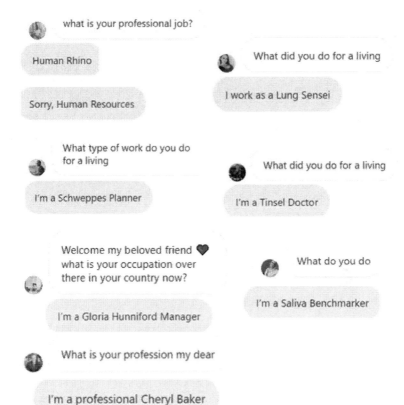

what is your professional job?

Human Rhino

Sorry, Human Resources

What did you do for a living

I work as a Lung Sensei

What type of work do you do for a living

I'm a Schweppes Planner

What did you do for a living

I'm a Tinsel Doctor

Welcome my beloved friend 🖤 what is your occupation over there in your country now?

I'm a Gloria Hunniford Manager

What do you do

I'm a Saliva Benchmarker

What is your profession my dear

I'm a professional Cheryl Baker

## SUGAR BABY

No, this isn't a term used for your wife when you want to sweeten your tea – a sugar baby is a person who receives cash, gifts or other benefits in exchange for being in an intimate relationship. Typically, the sugar baby is younger than the sugar daddy/mummy, and the relationship involves more than just sex. To be fair, it's always very nice when you randomly get this kind of message.

> Hello gorgeous how are You doing today sorry for stumping on your profile I'm here looking for a sugar baby who can keep me in company and I'll pay you $1,500 as your weekly allowance and pay up your bills can you do that for me darling...?

Not sure I want my profile stumped upon to be fair...

This kind of scam is normally all about blackmailing their victim. There is one advantage that women have and use—it's the desire of men to get a bit more intimate online[80]. A sugar baby will often build a relationship with you, and maybe even send you photos of them nude. Obviously, not them, images they've got from the internet. Here's some news: There is a very, very, very small section on the internet where you can see naked people. Just an FYI though, you cannot see any naked women on the internet before 9pm.

Although, flashback to that time that I convinced my grandmother that the internet closed at 4pm on Sunday. Sorry grandma, no medication for you! Anyway, in a sugar baby scam, a woman talks about sex, asks to send nudes, and sends hers even if you didn't ask for them. If you send them a naked photo, then they will blackmail you to give them money and if you don't, they will post the photo online.

---

[80] We all remember *that* photo of Dirty Den.

**ARE YOU ROBBIE VORTEX?**

This might be one of my favourite chapters of the book. Not only does it get very silly, very quickly – but we also get a little glimpse about what lengths scammers will go to. This chapter is as close to an episode of the television programme 'The Real Hustle' as it gets. Just without many of the elements of the television programme 'The Real Hustle'. You'll see what I mean.

This is Sandra. Despite just posting one photo, Sandra is following 1,990 people already. I would like to think that people are just browsing Instagram and then see Sandra, read her mantra on life and instantly follow her. *'People change, things to wrongful. Just remember, life goes on'*. As a life motto, it's up there with *'I like to cook with wine. Sometimes I even put it in the food'*, *'This house runs on love... and coffee'* and *'Oh look, it's prosecco o'clock'*. Sandra has really nailed the wise words vibe here. Anyway, Sandra decided to follow me. I followed back and then sent me the standard DM with a greeting.

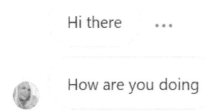

Thank-you Sandra for the message, but I'm afraid I was too busy trying to find someone on Instagram to make small talk with Sandra.

Are you Robbie Vortex?

Am Sandra please

One of the best things to do is to get scammers on the back front. I told Sandra that I was not on Instagram to speak to her. I was there to speak to a man known as Robbie Vortex.

Oh

I'm just here to find Robbie Vortex

I was here to find Robbie Vortex and I didn't need Sandra talking to me whilst I was on my mission to find Robbie. It seemed however that Sandra was interested in who Robbie was and why I needed to find him.

 Who is that?

Robbie Vortex is a man who I owe money to and I need to give it to him before Robbie Vortex's business associates find me and kill me

I knew that by dangling the word 'money', the scammer would sniff an opportunity and want to know more. Call it a hunch. I told Sandra I was looking for an old friend called Robbie Vortex as I owed him money.

So do you need my help

Let's talk and I will help you find him please

I knew it! After a bit more conversation, Sandra and I decided that we were both going to try and find Robbie Vortex, so that I could give Robbie the money I owed him. She sounded like female Sherlock Holmes. She-rlock Holmes if you will. I told Sandra that Robbie Vortex was an elderly gentleman, aged 99 years. Sandra seemed interested in helping me. Despite being 99 years old, Sandra asked where he works.

He worked at a casino called
'Johnny's Casino'

I sent a photo of Robbie Vortex to Sandra.

Obviously, this isn't a picture of Robbie Vortex. Eagle-eyed readers will know
that Robbie Vortex doesn't exist – but when you Google 'old man in distress' it
comes up with this photo. In reality, this is Albert Flick – a man who almost has
a name as good as Robbie Vortex. This picture of Albert was taken in court
when he was charged with killing a woman at the age of 77 years old[81].

Anyhoo, I told Sandra that I owed Robbie Vortex $50,000 and I had to give it to
him, or else his business associates. I did have one issue though.

I only have $48950 but I'm
hoping he will understand

 Don't worry

Sandra was good at quelling my fears. I knew that Robbie Vortex was a nasty
man, and as such if I didn't pay the full amount, there was a chance I would be
cut up into four pieces, garrotted and individual pieces of me sent to all corners

---

[81] It's actually a really grim story if you google it.

of the world. I told Sandra that when I contacted Robbie, he would give me a password, and only when that password was received, I would transfer the money to him.

> We have a special password that
> only me and him know

> When I see him I will give him
> the special password

So, the search was on. Despite not knowing anything about Sandra, including who she was and where she lived and only having spoken to her for about seven minutes, she seemed to be ever so helpful.

 I will have go to the North
Dakota and look for him myself

Stand aside Mother Teresa, Princess Diana and Rebekah Vardy, because we have a new best woman in the whole world. Sandra said she would travel to North Dakota to look for Robbie. However, I thought it would still be almost impossible trying to hunt down Robbie Vortex. The main reason being he was entirely fictitious. However, within about six minutes, I had another message from our favourite sleuth.

 I have good new for you

I told a friend at North Dakota
about this and he said he knows
him

Wow! What are the chances of this happening? I couldn't believe my eyes! We need to get Sandra on finding Shergar, Richey Edwards and the career of One True Voice. Sandra went into more detail on what she'd managed to find out.

He knows the son and the son is
a close friend of him

So he might he us to find him
okay

Look according to my friend he
said the som got very angry the
moment he heard about it

I was a little concerned that Robbie Vortex's son appeared to have anger
issues. What would Robbie's son say when he found out I didn't have the full
$50,000? How could I stop Robbie's son from getting angry? What was Robbie
Vortex's son's name? When would this bollocks come to an end? I had so many
questions. Despite asking all these questions to Sandra she had a clear head
and gave some sage advice.

Look take it easy

And just listen and do what he
will ask you to do

He can do any stupid is you
tried to challenge him

Apart from the last message, it was pretty good advice. At best, you could class
the last message as 'incoherent'. I had to try to keep telling myself that since
Sandra messaged me out the blue, the hunt for Robbie Vortex had certainly
picked up. Things were getting even hotter when I received a notification on
Instagram, telling me that I had a brand-new follower!

**robbie_vortex**

Sandra the scammer had created a new Instagram account and called it 'Robbie

Vortex'. On closer inspection, it turned out the Robbie Vortex's Instagram account only had one follower (yes, it was of course Sandra) and they hadn't posted any photos yet. Now, the sceptic in you might be thinking that a Nigerian scammer posing as a woman called Sandra has randomly created a new account in the name of Robbie Vortex to try and convince me that all this was real. To those people – I say, how dare you! How very dare you! Sandra told me to contact Robbie...

> That is the same instagram
> account

> But I try to reach him there he is
> not responding

> Try to reach him with the
> password between you guys

I decided to contact Robbie Vortex's son, so I sent him a DM. Sandra was right (again). Robbie Vortex's son was a ruddy lunatic, and I did my best to calm him down. I knew he had a temper. I knew that when he found out I was a little short of the money I owed his father, he would hit the bloody roof. So, I tried to appease him.

Oh my god

Is this who I think it is?

> Yes and stop asking me a lot of
> questions please

> Am not here to answer
> questions please

After a while, Robbie Vortex's son calmed down. We started to get to know each other. I was hoping that if I could form a friendship with him, I could get him on my side. As Del Boy once said to Rodney about DI Slater in an episode of Only Fools and Horses, 'I'd rather have him inside the tent pissing out, than outside the tent pissing in'. So, I tried to break the ice with some #GreatBants.

 Where have you been to

When I was 13 I went on a family trip to France. It was a long drive and my dad was grumpy by the end

The conversation with Robbie Vortex's son was cordial at best. He meant business. I meant business. So, we talked business.

 So is everything ready now?

I mean the money

I told him that I was ready to give him the money, after I was given the password. The password that Robbie Vortex and I had agreed on. I had already told Sandra this information. Robbie and I went way back, and this was the arrangement. I would exchange the money with his son if and when I received the password.

Well this is the son chatting you

And my dad didn't tell me about any password

Not wanting to anger him, I did tell him that in this scenario, if the password wasn't known – his father allowed me to give out a hint for the password.

> He said I could give you hint

> The hint is 'Foreskin of The West'

Even with the clue, it seemed that Robbie Vortex's son[82] still didn't know the password. However, what was clear was that he was getting pretty angry at not being sent the $50,000 that was owed to his father. Lord knows what he will say when I don't have the full amount of money. And Christ on a bike, what will he do when he finds out this is all a load of bollocks?!

> Please I told you he didn't tell me any password

> But if you are try to make this difficult then you are try to create a conflict between you and I

> And get ready for me if only you want to loose your life

It was all getting a bit tense. I was having my life threatened by a very angry fictitious man. I didn't know what to do. I had to check my life insurance to see if I had life insurance. I was just about to call Sheila's Wheels when I got a message from Sandra. Good old Sandra. You remember Sandra?

---

[82] I wish 'Sandra' had given Robbie Vortex's son a name as I sick of typing 'Robbie Vortex's son'.

Do you know something?

That his son is very dangerous
everyone is afraid of him

Sandra, to her credit, had warned me that Robbie Vortex's son was dangerous.
She was right. He was a ruddy nightmare. He was threatening me and my life. I
told Sandra all about this. She calmed me down. She told to make sure that I
cooperated with Robbie Vortex's son, and to do everything that he said.

For your own sake just please
listen to him and be safe

Are you saying I should just give
him the money?

Yes if you want your life please

Whilst I was replying to Sandra, and trying to remain clam, my phone kept
buzzing. You guessed it – it was the son of Robbie Vortex threatening me yet
again. Had he calmed? Had he buggery! He seemed even more angry than
before.

I will personal look for you

You have no where to enter I will
get you

You are try to make this difficult
for yourself right?

This guy really had to download the Calm app. I had to face facts. I had no way to enter. I was in a tricky position. The messages from Robbie Vortex's son kept on coming. It was quite frightening.

Am getting my guards ready for
you okay

What?! His guards? He had guards? Apparently, he had two guards. The one on the left couldn't stop sweating, whereas the other one smelt fresh. Because he was the Right Guard[83]. It turned out I was in big trouble. I was having all sorts of regrets. I should never have borrowed that fictional money from the fictional Robbie Vortex, and now I was being threatened by the fictional Robbie Vortex's son and his fictional guards. It was all getting a bit too much.

I went back to Sandra. I told Sandra that I could only give Robbie Vortex's son the money if he could provide the password that myself and Robbie Vortex himself had made up. Sandra asked what the password was.

It's just the password I have is
'RUBBERSOCKS' and I was told
not to give any money unless
they say that word

So, Sandra now had the password. But I made her promise not to tell a single soul. She promised. Not a single soul. Not one. Thirty seconds later, I got a message from Robbie Vortex's son.

ROBBERSOCKS

It was some sort of miracle. I started to suspect that Sandra might be working on the inside. Surely not? It was just an inkling, but I knew something wasn't right. Anyway, it turns out that the password was slightly incorrect too.

---

[83] Nope, I'm leaving that in.

What are you talking about hun

Do you think am here to play
fucking games with you?

Erm, bit rude mate. I told him again that the password was incorrect., He
spotted his mistake and quickly corrected it.

RUBBERSOCKS

Correct

That is the correct password

Finally, Robbie Vortex's son had given me the correct password. And so, as he
had given me the correct information, I now had to transfer the money over to
him. However, there was one more problem. I checked the information once
again.

I have just checked the
documents and it's turns out, it's
BOBBIE Vortex and not ROBBIE
Vortex.

So the money isn't for you

Have a good day.

You are mad okay

I supposed I owed the entire Vortex family an apology. It wasn't Robbie Vortex
at all, it was Bobbie Vortex who was in a whole different family. It didn't end

there though. You remember how the son of Robbie Vortex had an anger issue? Well, it turns out that anger doesn't dissipate when you tell him he's not going to get $50,000.

Send the money now

Because you are going to wanted all over the world

I was scared for my life here. I didn't want to be wanted all over the world. It turned out Robbie Vortex Jr was serious. He was deadly serious.

And for your information your picture is on social media being wanted

And is also with the FBI

I thought about the pickle I was in. What could I do to get the FBI off my back? Should I pay the money? Or should I just block Robbie Vortex's son and hope his guards, or the FBI catch up with me. As I was mulling the decision over, I had another Instagram message. This time it was from Sandra.

I just found a picture of you being wanted on social media

This is getting very serious

This was obviously very serious if Sandra has already seen on the internet that I am wanted. Maybe Sandra was constantly refreshing www.interpol.com. I didn't know, but one thing I did know was this was serious, and I had no option but to pay the $50,000.

Please send cashapp and PayPal information

$dinorusso69

 And this the PayPal

stevequerry@shaw.ca

I now had the information to make the payment. This was interesting. This was the first time I had ever received a scammers email and CashApp information. Full disclosure reader, I don't have a clue how CashApp works. It's something to do with money, and it's something to do with transfers, and something to do with apps. That's basically all I know. But I do know how PayPal works. As such, I had the scammers email address. They had given me the email address of stevequerry@shaw.ca. So, I thought I do my best Tosh Lines impression and do a bit of investigative work.

I typed the email address into Google and a couple of things came up. The email address was registered to a business – Bright World Restoration, a company from Edmonton in Canada that 'restore stainless steel trim, restore cars or anything to do with metal and plastic'. I found out that someone called Steve Querry had the owned the business for 23 years and recently he had set up a car show to raise funds for people who are recovering from strokes. Steve seemed like a nice guy. That was until I saw his Twitter[84] account. In his entire Twitter history, Steve had only sent out two tweets.

---

[84] X innit.

**Steve Querry** @stevequerry · 20 Dec 2020
The truth hurts hey Doug

**Steve Querry** @stevequerry · 20 Dec 2020
I guess the truth hurts hey Doug

I had an address in Edmonton in Canada, so I could hunt Steve Querry down. Why was a Nigerian scammer giving me the PayPal email address that was also affiliated with a car restoration business in Canada?

There was only one thing to do. I would get on a plane to Canada, head to Edmonton and speak to Steve Querry. Well, there was actually two things I could do. I could do the thing I have just mentioned, or I could just save my money and think about going on as plane to Canada to confront Steve Querry. So, that's what I did.

I thought about confronting Steve Querry. Well, I sent an email to Steve Querry. I wanted to tell him two bits of advice. The first was that the email address for his business had somehow been compromised and was being used by Nigerian scammers. The second piece of advice I wanted to give Steve was the basic rules of twitter and just to ask who the hell Doug is.

Sadly, this is where the story ends. There didn't seem to be any link between Steve Querry and the scammer, but it was a mystery why he had given that email address as their PayPal account.

If you are reading this Doug, please get it touch.

## LOTTERY

You wouldn't believe how much of a lucky guy I am! In the last three years since I started this Instagram account, I have been the winner of many Facebook lotteries, Instagram lotteries and competitions. I even once won second prize in a beauty competition. Yes, you are correct – I haven't entered a single one.

In this instance, the scammer will pose as someone who works for Instagram or Facebook and tell me on behalf of Mark Zuckerberg - the most amazing news; that I have won and won big baby! It might even be a message from the man himself – Mark Zuckerberg! Imagine getting a message from the real Mark Zuckerberg! Our friendly scammer will send over a copy of their company ID to build trust. The biggest amount I have ever won on these lotteries is $125,000,000. What's the catch I hear you ask? Take the money and run! Run! Run to Vegas! Take a private jet to Cannock and live the life of Lisa Riley!

Scammers also send through photos and videos of people who have also won to help legitimise the scam. There will be lots of photos of them holding a piece of card with some of the worst photoshopping you will ever see. Happy new year Tony!

However, as you can imagine, it's not as simple as that to claim your prize. To claim delivery of your special prize, you must pay a *small* delivery charge to Fedex to get your funds to you – which costs a measly $300. You don't pay directly to Fedex though, obviously. You pay the Fedex driver, who wants paying with an iTunes voucher. It's a novel approach, isn't it. But, what's $300 when you are going to get a cool, sweet $125m though, hey?! It's a drop in the ocean baby! Well, it's not... because obviously you never receive the $125m. Because the money doesn't exist. I hope you're catching on now.

The following interaction is not a lottery scam however but is part of a get rich quick scheme. It's just that I am the one trying to get rich.

**IT'S A PLAY, DARLING**

I had a message out of the blue from a scammer calling themselves 'Jade Cox'.
This is Jade.

## jade cox

jade_cox533 · Instagram

690 followers · 13 posts

You follow each other on Instagram

You both follow 1 person

Jade seems like a lovely person. She has 690 followers and has posted 13 times,
so it almost looks like the account might be genuine. Is she genuine? Let's find
out shall well. Jade started following me and when I #followedback, she sent
me a direct message.

Look at those upside-down emojis. She's obviously a little crazy. What a silly
sausage. How would I reply to this? A silly message back? A super serious
message?

Who is this?

Is this the police?

It was nice to be on the front foot. Jade was taken back a bit. She seemed
confused. She asked what I meant. I replied.

If so, it was an accident

I've still got the money

As soon as I messaged about money, Jade was interested in me. I couldn't understand why. But I think we all know why. I explained to Jade that I was part of a group that had just completed an armed robbery for two million pounds, and I was now awaiting instruction on what the next stage of the plan was. I asked Jade if she was messaging me to give me the next stage of the plan. It turned out she was. I asked her who she was.

Are you Pete the Meat?

 I'm jade the wise

Turns out Jade was playing along with this. Jade The Wise said she was part of the crew that was involved in the robbery.

Are you part of the crew?

 You can say that

What was your role in the crew?

 I'm your partner in crime ••••

I was liking Jade. I was liking her a lot. Straight away she was part of something big. And things were going to get really big for her. Jade also had a backstory on how she managed to be part of the crew.

I played along. Alberto was apparently one of the crew too, so if he let Jade be part of the group, then I was fine with her being in. The relationship was blossoming.

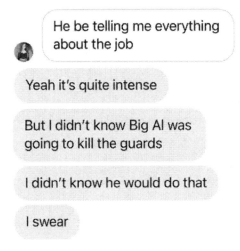

Oh dear. The robbery had gone slightly awry. It turns out that Big Al had killed someone. I explained to Jade that no-one was supposed to get hurt, and that it was an accident. Jade understood. She was part of the crew after all.

Jade was part of the crew. I trusted her. She asked what the next stage of the plan was. It seemed she wanted to move on to the next stage, and get the money owed to her.

What are you doing rn

I'm waiting on the next part of the plan

Ian the Fish and Salty Donald are coming over with the guns and then we move to stage 2

If you're going to do a job, you need to make sure you have your trusted friends with you. I trusted Ian the Fish and Salty Donald. I also trusted Jade the Wise and Big Al. These were all part of the crew that pulled off one of the biggest robberies! Two million big ones split amongst us. Nothing could go wrong. But Jade was getting itchy on us all.

You've not send me my share on the first operation

I need it

Jade was trying to get her share of the money now. This wasn't the plan we agreed. Damnit Jade, we all agreed on the plan prior to the robbery, and she was trying to ruin things. I explained to her what the plan was.

Big Al says we split it at the end

That was always the plan

Jade was adamant there was a change of plan and that she should be paid now. But I knew that Big Al, the big boss and esteemed leader was the only one that would change the plan. I was tempted to speak to Big Al and ask him what the heck was going on.

> You should PayPal me my share when the big A1 tell you what next to do

I liked Jade even more when she called Big Al 'big A1', like the boss is a giant piece of paper. What a card she was. Not only this, but she was also pretty forward in what she wanted.

> Send me 2000 on PayPal now

> I need it to get my license on some

We now knew what Jade wanted. It was $2,000 via PayPal. If you think about it, that's only 0.1% of the total we got from the robbery. Say what you want about Jade, but she certainly wasn't pricing herself out of this deal. I was starting to think that the 'Jade the Wise' moniker was quite ironic.

But I was unsure what to do now? Do I give Jade the money? The plan was always to split the money at the end. There was only thing to do. I created a private chat and added Big Al to the chat to sort this matter out. The problem with this of course was that Big Al didn't exist. Well, he didn't exist.

Until now.

I quickly created a brand-new Instagram account and called myself Big Al. For reasons unknown even to me, I thought that Big Al should have the profile picture of 80's comedian Jasper Carrott.

 big_al_big_al

Big Al entered the group chat.

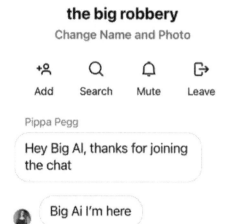

## the big robbery

Change Name and Photo

+o Add   Q Search   ⌂ Mute   ⇨ Leave

Pippa Pegg

Hey Big Al, thanks for joining the chat

Big Ai I'm here

You have to give it to Jade; she was game for this. I like scammers who try something different, and here was Jade trying to tell people she was part of a two-million-pound robbery and trying to cash in. Back to the story, Big Al told Jade that there was already a plan in place and as agreed, we would split the cash at the end.

jade cox

Well I know that the plan but I needed the reason and I told you about it already Ai

Don't do this to me now big boss

Jade was standing up to Big Al, the big boss. She was playing with fire, because as we all know Big Al doesn't take any crap from anyone. Jade then started sending direct messages to Big Al telling me/him that she needed the money for a special assignment. Big Al asked Jade what her actual role in the robbery was. Bless you Jade.

I was your informat and now you've forgotten so fast

That made sense. Jade had been the informant and wanted to be paid. As the

194

conversation continued, there was starting to be a little tension between me (Pippa Pegg) and Jade. I got the feeling Jade was trying to drive a wedge between me and Big Al. Big Al asked Jade who employed her, and she said Carlos was her boss. As we all know, Big Al and Carlos knew each other from when they were doing 'Twenty to ten in the pen'[85], and Big Al reminisced about his past crimes with Carlos like they had just connected on Facebook in 2010.

To be honest, this was quite the admin challenge, switching accounts, pretending to two different people. But it was about to get worse. A lot worse.

jade cox

> I will tell Carlos about pegg I'm
> sure he's going to take you out

Jade was trying to push me Pippa out of this group. I had to reply. We had been such a tight group of robbers until Jade showed up.

Pippa Pegg

> What? Take me out??

> What do you u mean?

jade cox

> As the big Ai he will tell you
> about the plan b

Was Jade trying to oust me from the group? What was going on? What would Big Al say to this? It was all getting a bit tense for my liking. However, Big Al replied.

> I'll tell you Pegg

> Plan B is we take the money and
> we end up killing all the rats that
> we don't like

---

[85] Prison innit.

Jade continued to push buttons.

> Well you tel him now I hope he
> doesn't rat us out and he
> ending up having all the money
> all to him self

I wasn't a rat, but it sure looked like Jade was saying I was a rat. I pleaded with Jade to tell Big Al the truth.

Pippa Pegg

I wouldn't

Please

I'm not a rat

Tell him Jade

Tell him I ain't no rat

Pippa asked Jade to tell Big Al that I wasn't a rat. This robbery had gone so well (apart from Big Al killing the guard obvs[86]) but it seemed we were falling apart at the seams. Jade continued to drop group chat grenades.

jade cox

> Pegg is not a rat but if he
> messed up the plan I believe he
> won't be happy with the
> consequences

This was getting awkward pretty quickly and Pippa told Big Al that she didn't

---

[86] Soz to his family.

trust Jade. That seemed to be the straw that broke the camel's back, and Jade wanted Pippa out of this business arrangement for good.

Say, whaaaaaat?!?! How could she do this to me? How dare she! Surely Big Al wouldn't believe this nonsense. The relationship between Pegg and Big Al went back a long way and sure he would have her back. Surely?

Oh heck. Were Pippa Pegg's days numbered? This wasn't looking good. Jade was certainly looking forward to Pegg's impending demise.

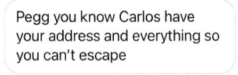

Jade was trying to put the fucking boots in! What the hell Jade?! I'm sure Big Al would see through this charade and make sure it was all OK. Surely? Big Al replied. Hopefully he would help quell the situation.

> I can do even better than that

> Hey Pegg...you know that Little Tina lives close to you?

> Well she might be paying you a visit now if you know what I mean

This was not looking good for Pippa Pegg. Not looking good at all. Jade had double crossed Pegg, but I suppose there was still time for Jade to make things better.

> I'm sorry pegg you've been good to the team

Jade was ruthless. Ruthless. She reminded me of Eammon Holmes when his wife eventually leaves him[87]. It seemed that Pippa Pegg was living on borrowed time. Pippa explained that she didn't have the money, as per the plan it was being dealt with by someone else. Those excuses were falling on deaf ears. Pegg sounded desperate.

> Please wait

> Oh god there is someone at the door

> Please

> Please

Then silence. Silence from Jade. Silence from Big Al. More importantly, silence from Pippa Pegg. What was going on? The silence was deafening. Suddenly, Little Tina entered the chat.

---

[87] Her name is Ruth. Keep up, I'm not explaining them all.

littl.etina312

> Dead

> Job completed

Little Tina had killed Pippa Pegg! OMG! A huge development I think we can all agree. You are correct reader; the Instagram silence was actually being filled by me creating another Instagram profile called 'Little Tina'. Honestly, the admin involved in this charade was ridiculous. Back to the story, even Jade seemed a bit surprised by it all.

> You killed him? Tina

> That's all messed up Tina

It turns out Jade does have a heart after all. But, if I am honest, it's a little late for all this. Big crimes have big consequences, and sadly Pippa Pegg was a consequence that got taken out. Was Tina starting to get cold feet on all of this? Was she starting to have regrets? Was she bollocks!

> Tina watch the way you text me

> Carlos is with me

Tina, as feisty as ever, was still very much part of this and wanting her money. She again started asking for the $2,000 owed to her in the robbery. Big Al again informed her that the plan was still the same.

Once the money from the robbery was in his hands, then the money would be split equally between everyone involved in the robbery. There was one person missing from this group and that was the man who had the money from the robbery. Big Al added Medium Dennis to the group chat.

big_al_big_al added mediumdennis199

I was now portraying four different characters and in the space of 30 minutes had created an extra three Instagram accounts. I felt like I was in the Instagram version of The Nutty Professor. That figure I mentioned earlier around 10% of all Instagram accounts being fake was being pushed to its limit.

Back to the story. Medium Dennis explained that he didn't know many of the people in the group, but as agreed, he had the money and was on his way to meet Big Al to deliver it. In fact, it was lovely for Medium Dennis to get introduced to everyone in the group chat. Even Tina was introducing people to him.

> Dennis Tina is new
>
> But she's good with her job

But all of a sudden, there was another plot twist. As it was becoming more and more difficult to switch between Instagram profiles and characters, Jade had started messaging the recently deceased Pippa Pegg. I'm not sure why. I presumed to see if she was actually dead. Little Tina wasn't impressed.

> Why is Jade texting Pegg's phone?
>
> I'm making sure he's dead
>
> Tina need to be monitored

We all agreed that now everyone was here, and the money was safe with Medium Dennis, we could split the money. Jade agreed. It was time to bring an end to this ridiculous scenario. As he had the money, Medium Dennis gave the instructions to all.

mediumdennis199

Okay. Earlier today, before the robbery, you were all given envelopes

Those envelopes will have a piece of paper on them

That piece of paper has a single letter on it

Please take the paper from your envelope and tell me the letter

Jade said that she didn't have an envelope. Medium Dennis replied and asked her if her role was as an informant. Jade confirmed. Medium Dennis said if that was the case, she wouldn't have an envelope. One by one, the group revealed the letters contained in the envelope.

mediumdennis199

I have 2 envelopes

The first letter is A

littl.etina312

I have L

One says A and the other says Y

mediumdennis199

We need to put these together

So we have A LA YE

We had spelled out the word ALAYE, and now for 'Jade the Wise', it was clear that the whole thing had been a complete waste of time, and we knew Jade was a Nigerian scammer.

The game was up for everyone. Or was it? It was time for everyone to come forward and congratulated themselves on a wonderful performance. This had all been an Instagram play, and boy, our actors were very congratulatory about each other.

That was a pleasure

mediumdennis199

Many thanks to everyone who took part in the play tonight

littl.etina312

Dennis you were wonderful darling

It was a wonderful atmosphere. All the actors were patting each other on the back for a job well done. Everyone seemed very happy with themselves. Well, everyone except one person.

Did you not like this Jade?

Darling why not?

jade cox

Well I'm hurting financially that's why I play along

It seems Jade didn't appreciate being part of the play. She called us all a

Nigerian word that translated as something that wouldn't be allowed on UK television before 9pm. Even Pippa Pegg herself, made an appearance back from the dead.

Pippa Pegg

I AM ALIVE!!!

Lol

This was Abso wonderful

jade cox

No it wasn't

Everyone's a critic these days, aren't they? Medium Dennis[88], Big Al[89], Pippa Pegg[90] and Little Tina[91] were all congratulating each other, and you know what these actors are like – they just wouldn't shut up.

Pippa Pegg

I just tried to get into that character. Once I knew her story, she was lovely to play

Lovely to tread the digital boards again to be honest. Twas a bloody pleasure.

Loved playing the big boss too.

I was in the background of The Bill once

---

[88] Me
[89] Also me.
[90] Again, me.
[91] Yes, me again.

Whether it was the mention of The Bill, or the fact that we were all just talking absolute bollocks, Jade had heard enough. She once again called us all a name you mainly hear in a Guy Ritchie film and blocked us all.

Look out for a six-part Netflix documentary on this adventure next September.

## A NEW JOB OPPORTUNITY

Life can get you down sometimes – but you never know when good luck is going to slap you right in the mush. Especially when you're on the world wide web of opportunity. So, when I got this message, little did I know it would change my life forever.

> If $1000 was sent too your Cash
> App for free without you paying
> any money

A pretty normal sort of message really. Just a stranger contacting you to let you know they will give you $1,000. After asking them what the ruddy heck was going on, and queried if they had sent the message in error – I received the following:

> My company is running a
> giveaway to interested people
> who just want to refer more
> people to sign up. They're
> actually on their anniversary.

What a great company! Maybe those big tech CEO suit wearers should take a leaf out of this (so far) unnamed company and start thinking outside the box! What a great idea, to dish out some dollar to random Instagram accounts simply because it's the anniversary of the company being set-up. This is the kind of business strategy that the likes of John Menzies, Woolworths and Lunn Polly[92] should have adopted, and maybe they wouldn't be on the scrap heap now. After finding out that the (still unnamed) company was celebrated its two-year anniversary (congrats guys!), I wanted to be part of it, and I had to find out if there were any jobs going.

---

[92] I was going to add Wilko to this list, but it's still too raw.

> I don't suppose you've got any jobs going at your company?

 What do you mean sorry

> I'm looking for a new job and it seems your company is doing really well so wondered if you had any jobs

Well, you don't ask, you don't get. The worst thing they could say was 'No', right? After some conversation, I finally found out some good news - they had some job openings! Was my professional outlook about to see a change? This could be the change I was looking for! Pensions! Company car! Shareholder dividends! It was all very exciting. So, I quickly sent over my CV to see if my experiences matched the ones they were looking for.

## Pippa Pegg

Address: 999 Letsbe Avenue, Rozzer Town, London
Email: pippapegg35@g.com

---

### PROFESSIONAL EXPERIENCE

---

**Driving Nemesis – Alton Towers**　　　　　　　　　　　　　　　　July 2017 – present

- I currently am one of the drivers for the white knuckle ride Nemesis at Alton Towers.
- This ride involves driving around corners really fast, going 'loop the loop' on a number of occasions, and also braking when the ride is finished.
- Previously, I worked as an operator for the Runaway Mine Train ride at Alton Towers where I was 30% responsible for their catchphrase 'Choo Choo Since '92'.
- I used to also say 'Exit on the left please' after the ride, but that responsibility got taken away from me, when I once – instead of saying 'Exit on the left please', I said 'Exit on the right please'.

**Drayton Manor Park**　　　　　　　　　　　　　　　　　　　　　January 2014 – July 2017

- This role involved just walking around the theme park pretending to be a member of the public, so it looked like there was more members of the public at the theme park, because normally there usually wasn't many members of the public at the theme park.
- Had the idea to rebrand 'Drayton Manor Park' into 'Drayton Manor Park and Zoo' as Drayton Manor Park had a lot of land that they couldn't afford to build new rides on. So, I had the bright idea to chuck a few rabbits in there, and call it a zoo.
- Responsible for having the idea of a log flume and river rapids ride at Drayton Manor Park when I once spent the day at Alton Towers.

I'd hope I'm the only person who has the line 'Choo Choo Since '92' in their CV. I'd hoped that my skills and previous employment would leave me in good stead to be a great fit for this (yup, still unnamed) company. After driving Nemesis for a number of years, I needed a new challenge and it seemed that this (will it ever be named?) unnamed company, might be the perfect fit for me and my career goals.

> What jobs have you got going? I'm looking for something in middle management ideally, I've o project management experience, stakeholder management and event planning too.
>
> 93

The scammer finally told me the name of the company. It was very imaginatively named 'HHHH'. I needed to find out a bit more about HHHH, so went on to LinkedIn to find out more about their business strategy, their goals, their corporate social responsibility pledges.

It turns out there actually is a company called 'Hhhh' on LinkedIn., and they are a (very small) Law Enforcement firm in Doha, Qatar. Could it be these guys? I would suggest that the real 'Hhhh' company hires a Social Media Manager, because currently on their 'About' page on LinkedIn, it genuinely just says the following 'Ybhcgg'. Anyway, I needed to know more about HHHH.

> What does HHHH stand for?

> The you like the work

> Acronyms not your strong suit?

Sadly, I think myself and HHHH were on separate pages. I was looking for a new job, a new career, a new fresh start... and the person I was talking to... was trying to get to change my password on my Instagram account to their email address.

---

93 A spelling mistake in a job application? Oh, James!

If you are done you can send me a screenshot

Of the presentation? You only asked me to do it 10 minutes ago!

Have you added the Gmail

Is that question 2 of the interview? That sounds like a puzzle. I have to say this is quite a thorough interview

That was a pretty intense interview. It seemed quite unorthodox, but I think I got through it. Like any job interview, it was important I asked my questions to them. It was just as important that HHHH was the right fit for me that I was for them.

Does the company have free parking?

Dress down Friday?

You know what would be good? If the canteen did egg in soup

Sadly, the representative from HHHH seemed quite confused.

I don't understand

It basically a soup. For example, tomato soup. Then just add a poached egg.

As the interview finished, we both got on with our day. But to be fair, I felt like I had a great chance for this vacancy at Hungry Hippos Headquarters in Holland (make up your own mind as to what HHHH stands for). So, I thought I would get in contact with HHHH and find out the status of my job application.

I know you've probably had lots of applications about the vacancy, but when do you think I'll hear back?

What do you mean

Playing it cool. I understand

It felt like I was going for a job interview at MI5, they were being so secretive!

Also – shout out to my friend who about 15 years ago applied for a job at MI5 when she saw a job advert in The Guardian. They liked her application, and she had a telephone interview where she excelled. MI5 invited her down to London on the train, expenses paid, and asked her to do a psychometric test. She did really well. She also had to have part of her hair tested for drugs. After all this, they then invited back down to London again for a formal interview with them. Again, all expenses paid. After all this testing, the first question they asked her was why she was applying for a job with MI5. Without blinking, she replied to the interview panel 'I really enjoyed watching the TV show Spooks'.

She didn't get the job.

Anyway, after going back and forth with the representative from HHHH – it turned out to be great news! I got the job! I got the (still yet untitled) job! Yes!

A new career for me! My mum would be so proud. Thanks to HHHH for giving taking a chance on me! However, still at this point, I had questions. A lot of questions. Salary, pension, benefits, start date, references, hybrid working status, cycle to work scheme. The usual kind of thing.

> Bruh! Have anyone ever tell you
> that you talk a lot?

I loved the fact I was being called 'bruh' by Human Resources before I had even started the job. I just loved the informality of HHHH. The kind of place that has a poster in the canteen saying 'You don't have to be crazy to work here, but it helps' – which, to be frank, I am all for! I'm all for these cool, hipster style thought-cloud workspaces. Despite being told I talk too much; I kept going with my incessant (and needless) questions.

> Can you talk about your pension
> scheme?

> I see you don't need it

> We really do. There's going to
> be a pension black hole in years
> to come. We really need to save
> for our collective futures.

I had so many questions for my new friends at HHHH. I asked what vegetarian options does the canteen provide before 9am? I'd like to think we all like to get a get a soy-based meal prior to starting work.

> You don't need it

Yes, I do. If I decide to follow a broadly vegan diet, I need to know where I can get my foods that will give me the necessary nutrients to keep me working at 100% throughout the day. Hence my other question about protein balls, turmeric shots and tofu supplements.

> You don't need it

Yes, I do. Especially when these date-filled protein balls aren't cheap you know. Especially when shopping from Holland & Barrett[94].

> You don't need it

Yes, I do. Maybe HHHH was not the right company for me. It seemed such a good place on the outside. HHHH was willing to give strangers money because they were celebrating their two-year anniversary. I spoke to friends; I spoke to family. I slept on it for a couple of hours. I then messaged HHHH back and I told them that I was rescinding my job application.

> You don't need it

I know. That what I said.

Then I got blocked. What a sHHHHame.

---

[94] Who have disappointingly never rebranded to 'Netherlands & Barrett'.

**JOBS – PART 2**

Here's more of the jobs that I have said I have had. Each one of them more odd sounding than the last. Not one of the jobs I said I was questioned.

 What do you do for a living

I'm a Panna Cotta Cabinet

 What is your occupation?

I work as a Cornetto Dehumidifier

 What your occupation

I work as a Fanta Mechanic

 What are you doing for a living

I work as a Horlicks Shatter

 What do you do for a living

I work as a Equine Decider

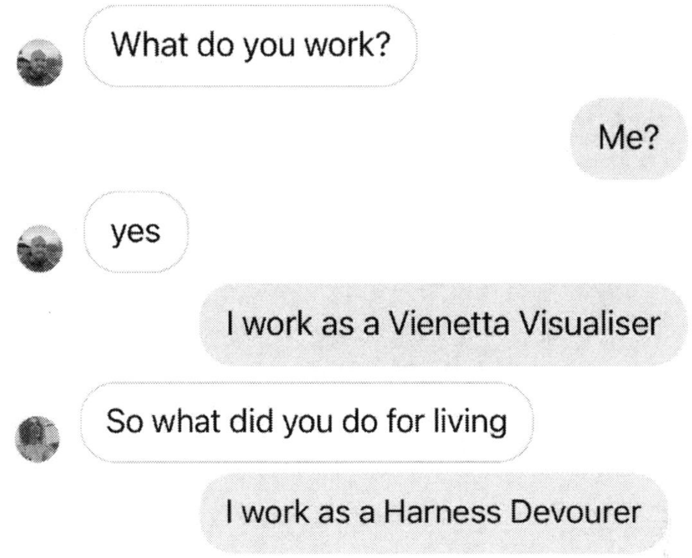

What do you work?

Me?

yes

I work as a Vienetta Visualiser

So what did you do for living

I work as a Harness Devourer

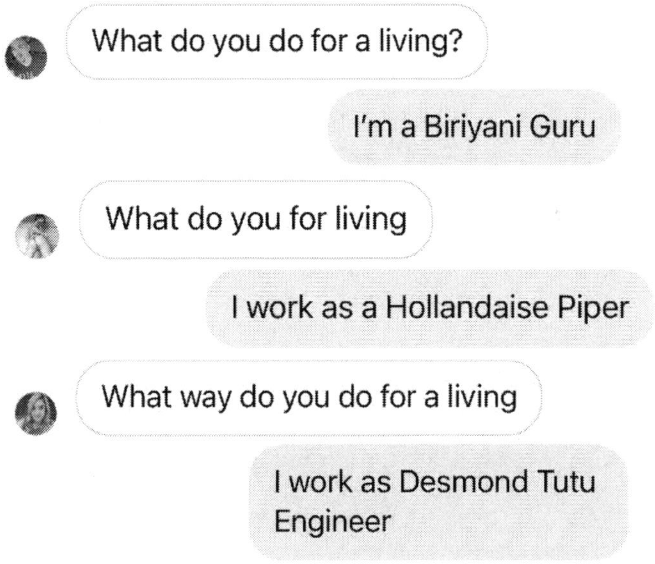

What do you do for a living?

I'm a Biriyani Guru

What do you for living

I work as a Hollandaise Piper

What way do you do for a living

I work as Desmond Tutu Engineer

What do for a living to take care of yourself?

I'm a Tapas and Blizzard Specialist

What are you doing for a living

I work as Tizer Enthusiast

What did you do for a living

I work as a Tempura Delighter

Wow nice place 👍
What do you do for work

I work as a Netball Sleuth

What are you doing for a living?.

I work as Ciabatta Mechanic

What do you do for a living

I work as a Kula Shaker Unifier

What did you do for a living?

I work as a Tandori Officer

## BITCOIN

It's the bitcoin scam. Ah, your friend and mine, the old bitcoin. Now, for cool hip millennials like me who have their cauliflower ear to the ground and say words like 'cowabunga' 'wazzzzzzup' and 'I miss Tandy' - we know all about what bitcoin is. But for those super dweebs who may not know, bitcoin is a digital currency. This means you can't really see it; can't drink it and you can't take it out for a walk. That's my understanding of it anyway.

I've lots of messages from people asking me if I have heard of bitcoin mining. It's pretty easy to understand. For those grandads who are unaware - Bitcoin mining is the process of adding transaction records to Bitcoin's public ledger of past transactions or blockchain. This ledger of past transactions is called the block chain as it is a chain of blocks. The block chain serves to confirm transactions to the rest of the network as having taken place. Bitcoin nodes use the block chain to distinguish legitimate Bitcoin transactions from attempts to re-spend coins that have already been spent elsewhere. I hope you're taking notes, they'll be an exam at the end of the book.

Scammers would message me asking me to invest in bitcoin. They promised me huge wealth. They said I would triple my investment in just 30 minutes. Invest $500, your return is $1,500. Invest $1,000? Sure, your return is $3,000. Nothing can go wrong. Oh, hang on. Of course, it can. Because you will invest and never hear from these people again and your money will be gone forever. This kind of scam usually attempts the victim to invest as much money as possible. They believe it's an investment and their return will be huge, and I spoke to one scammer who said he once fleeced $10,000 from someone in a single transaction. More on him later...

## TWO MORE PEOPLE

The next scammer on the list is a guy who goes by the name of Ravi. Ravi in an investment guy. He's all about the dollar. He's searching for people on Instagram to help invest money with him. The plan is we will all get rich. Ravi messaged me. He told me of his plan. We were all going to get rich, really quick!

> The idea is, building a solid capital foundation for beginners by helping out with trades while they watch, learn and at same time build their capital and I'm entitled to get 10% of your total profit as commission. The offer by the way is limited, I'm giving this offer free to 20 of my followers today, you are so lucky to be the 18th person, so it won't be available sometime after now as we won't be able to accommodate a very high population of investors.

It's a pretty standard investment opportunity. You traded your money based on recommendations from Ravi who would take 10% of the profits, and you get to keep the rest! Nothing can go wrong. I was privileged to be contacted (out of the blue) by Ravi. I didn't know him, but when a stranger contacts you on Instagram talking about how you can both get rich quick, you listen. The good news was that I was the 18th person out of 20 people that Ravi contacted. I was very lucky indeed.

> I'm 18th! Wow I was really lucky

> Can you let me know the other 19 people who are benefitting?

I was looking to congratulate the other 19 people on being part of this investment opportunity. Maybe we could all get involved with a WhatsApp group? Call it 'Investment Legends' and brag about how much dollar we're making!

> For me personally, I've found
> success with trading off crypto
> ... and that helped me generate
> more than $200,000 in trading
> profits during the months of
> 2021/2022

Wow! Imagine making more than $200,000 during those well-known months of 2021 and 2022. We were dealing with a professional here! But I didn't just want to get rich on my own. I wanted to get my friends involved in the investment opportunity and make sure they weren't missing out.

After a back and forth with Ravi, it turns out that he hadn't found a 19th and 20th person for this investment opportunity. Well, it's lucky he contacted me - because I was only too eager to help! I had to think about which two of my great mates would be best to take advantage of this once in a lifetime opportunity.

> Ok here is the details for
> number 19. I know this guy. He's
> a great guy and is always up for
> a bargain. Try @nigel_farage.

I knew Nigel Farage would be interested. He's an honest guy with a nose for financial savviness. Ravi seemed keen too.

> I just followed him

After Ravi had started the former UKIP Leader, Ravi asked me who the 20th person was. For me, there was only one person it could be.

> Contact @ladbabyofficial

Nigel Farage and LadBaby. What a couple. One is an unscrupulous, fame hungry, megalomaniac, loved by the lowest intellect across the United Kingdom, parading himself as a man of the people.

And the other is called Nigel[95].

Ravi was now following both Farage and LadBaby. I was however concerned that he had no idea who LadBaby was.

> Have you ever heard of Ladbaby?

 Nope

This was a little disconcerting. I thought everyone had heard of LadBaby and his pastry-based antics. It turns out that writing ditties about sausage rolls and groping women in nightclubs[96] wasn't enough to endear himself to Ravi, so I had to introduce Ravi to the world of LadBaby. If we were all going to be investment-based bezzies, it was only right that you know who you're investing with.

> Have you heard Ladbaby's song 'Sausage Roll Sausage Roll Sausage Roll', it's quite the tune

 Let me check it out bro

So, while Ravi was listening to *We Built This City (On Sausage Rolls)'* (#1 in the UK charts, #47 in the US Rock Charts), *'I Love Sausage Rolls'* (#1 in the UK charts, #100 in the Australian charts), *'Don't Stop Me Eatin'* (#1 in the UK charts, #12 in the New Zealand Hot Press), *'Sausage Rolls For Everyone'* (#1 in the UK charts, #48 in the Australian charts) and *'Food Aid'* (#1 in the UK charts

---

[95] Zing.
[96] Allegedly.

and #38 in the New Zealand Hot Press) I was planning on how to spend my profits.

After a while, Ravi got back to me.

Nice it's really awesome

The song is really good to me
bro

After begrudgingly accepted that I was responsible for increasing LadBaby's Spotify royalties by £0.0007, it was at least good to see that Ravi had found a new favourite artist. However, there was still no news from Nigel Farage. Ravi messaged me to ask if there was an update from the two potential investors.

So any new from LadBaby??

Well I think he's still filming hilariously staged videos playing pranks on his 'long suffering' wife in the short term. But expect a flaky festive favourite tune at the end of the year

I told Ravi that I had contacted my best mate LadBaby to tell him to get involved in this wonderful investment opportunity. Ravi, for some reason, seemed a bit off and asked me to share the messages between LadBaby and I.

Can you send me a screenshot of your chat with him if you don't mind me asking

Now, this obviously put me in a bit of a quandary. I have to be honest with you here reader. The fact of the matter is, I don't actually know LadBaby and therefore I hadn't been in contact with him about being part of this business venture. However, I didn't want to lose out on this investment. So, I had a conversation with LadBaby[97] which was definitely real[98] and sent him the screenshot of the conversation.

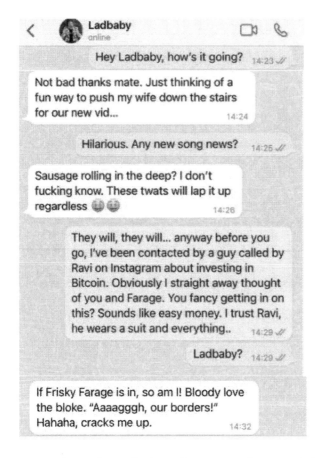

So, Ravi knew that LadBaby and I were in. All we needed was Nigel and we would have the 20 people needed to make sure this investment went down. Even Ravi was believing it too.

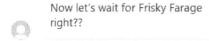

Now let's wait for Frisky Farage right??

It made me so happy that someone in Nigeria was calling Nigel Farage 'Frisky'.

---

[97] My mate Nick.
[98] Not at all.

Try as Ravi could, he did not receive any Instagram messages back from LadBaby or Nigel Farage. Which I think we can all agree, is a real shame. And so, without Frisky Farage and L to the B, it was just left to me to invest with Ravi. I was ready to go. See you later UK. Hello Barbados. There's was just one question from Ravi on how to make the investment.

> Do you have any bitcoin wallet
> ??

I have a leather wallet.

My mum got it from TK Maxx. It had a sticker on it to say the price in store was below the recommended retail price.

And with that, Ravi had finally had enough.

> Your really stupid

After the most ironic of insults, Ravi blocked me. I sometimes think of the scammer behind Ravi. Did he really listen to the sounds of LadBaby? If so, did he really enjoy it? Did he tell his Nigerian friends and family about LadBaby? Had I just created a monster? Is there a chance that LadBaby by some massive fluke is just about to take the Nigerian pop world by storm? A cover of Culture Club's classic renamed as 'Scammer Chameleon' anyone?

Luckily for LadBaby or the poor song writers that do his work for him, I've already re-written the lyrics.

**Scammer Chameleon**
Scammer, scammer, scammer, scammer, scammer chameleon
You con and go; you con and go.
Scamming would be easy if your victims were all like me.
I'm LadBaby. I'm LadBaby.

Every day you're in denial (denial)
You're a scammer, that is final.

Every day you're in denial (denial)
You're a scammer, that is final.

I'm a man (a man) without conviction (due to shocking laws around
international fraud)
I'm a (Nigerian) man (a man) who doesn't know.
How to sell (to sell) bitcoin mining
You scam and go; you scam and go.

Scammer, scammer, scammer, scammer, scammer chameleon
You con and go; you con and go.
Scamming would be easy if your victims were all like me.
I'm LadBaby. I'm LadBaby.

## BITCOIN VIDEO

Following on from the bitcoin scam, is the imaginatively named 'bitcoin video' scam. In this scenario, scammers force Instagram users to film hostage-style videos instructing their followers to participate in the Bitcoin scheme.
If someone has been the victim of the bitcoin con or ambassador scam (more on this later), scammers will promise to give their money back if they film themselves promoting the scam, they have just fallen victim to! After filming the video, however, the scammer posts the video to the victim's Instagram account and sends the video to their friends and posts it from their profile to try and scam others.

Victims are forced to film a video such as *"Hey you guys, I just got back from a long day of work, but Brian just helped me invest $1,000 and got me back $8,500. What an amazing way to end the day, and I feel so blessed and appreciative for this process. It's guaranteed. I suggest doing it."*

In these instances, the scammer tells the account holder to make a video promoting the Bitcoin scam in exchange for access to the account. The scammer obviously doesn't give access back, but instead posts the video on that person's account, so it encourages their friends and family to take part.
If you ever see my real Instagram account, and you see me posting a video of me talking about the benefits of a new Breville sandwich toaster, please don't feel that I've been scammed by Breville. I'm just big into sandwich toasties, and we all know Breville is king. Yeah, I'm looking at you Breville Ultimate Deep Fill VST082 Sandwich Toaster (Black).

## ILLUMINATI

> Illuminati invitation:
> Based the membership criterion of the Illuminati, we find you are of great interest in possession of a good mastery of manual dexterity and academic proficiency. With this, we look at you as the class that will be the platform for which you stand to meet the wealthy people who can raise you to wealth, power, fame and glory. I strongly recommend that you join us in the Illuminati. Joining us you become wealthy and live the life you desire. Do you accept the offer?

Who doesn't want to be part of the illuminati? Who doesn't want to be part of an organisations that conspires to control world affairs, by masterminding events and planting agents in government and corporations in order to gain political power and influence and to establish a New World Order[99]?

It certainly beats being a member of Costco. Invitations to the illuminati also come with a huge amount of money, power and a lovely truck (for some reason, it's always a truck!). Who would say no to all this power? Starting a discussion with the illuminati is always an interesting one. They speak about having conversations with 'The Grand Master' – a name that suggests they are the final boss on Shinobi.

The only thing stopping you from joining this illustrious organisation is just a few details – your name, address, phone number, email, social security number, date of birth, picture of driving license. Oh, and a few hundred dollars to get your truck delivered. I don't need to tell you that if you give them money, you don't get the truck and unlimited wealth.

## MUSE SCAMS

This is the double yolk of scams. You don't get it very often, but you feel very lucky when it happens. You'll get a direct message saying that they are a

---

[99] Not the one Eric Bischoff put together.

budding artist, and they really like your profile photo. They like your profile photo so much that they want the opportunity to draw you and hang the picture in a local museum. Who wouldn't want their picture hanging in a local museum? I remember going to the MC Hammer Museum once. Security was really strict. You can't touch anything.

Anyway, after agreeing to having your picture drawn, the scammer will then talk about having a buyer lined up ready and waiting to buy the painting when it is ready, and they will go 50/50 on the profit of the drawing. What can go wrong? Well, if you made it this far so far, you'll know everything will go wrong. Obviously, the artist doesn't exist, the museum doesn't exist, and the buyer of the painting doesn't exist. Not only that, but the art supplies themselves don't even exist. Which is why the artist also asks for money to buy them. You would think that an artist would have the necessary supplies to complete a painting, but sadly not. It is a bit like booking an Uber, but also paying for the car's MOT before you get in the vehicle.

## META-SCAMMERS ON META

This is one I like. Scammers thinking outside the box. Sometimes you will get a message out of the blue from someone who has recently followed you asking you if you are following a certain person. They will tell you to be very careful because the person is a scammer, and they have reported their account to Instagram to get it closed down. They'll tell you they are messaging all their followers to inform them to be very careful because the person is a scammer and not to give them any money. This is all very helpful I'm sure you'll agree. What a nice, considerate person you're probably thinking. Score one for the good guys. Just before you start completing their OBE application form, let me give you this bombshell – that person is also a scammer! Yeah, you heard me right. Shut the front door. Now, shut the back door. Thanks there was a heck of a draught.

As I stated before, scammers are looking to build trust as quickly as possible. There's no better way to build trust than bonding on exposing a scammer on Instagram. Once that trust has been built, more traditional conversations can happen. You know the conversations we're talking about: What do you do for a living? What is your job? Are you single? You get the idea.

**JOBS – PART 3**

The fact that I have spoken to so many scammers over the years means I have spent a lot of my time making up the most ridiculous names for occupations. Here's yet more silly job titles that to me and you sound like about nonsense.

What do you do for work

I work as a Beetroot Ultra

What do you do for a living

I'm a Fondue Descendant

What did you do for a living

I work as a Vulva Decider

What are you doing for a living

I work as a Danube Surpriser

what do you do for a living

I supply harbours to dogs

what is your occupation

I'm a Silhouette Destroyer

What are you doing for living??

I'm a Thyroid Swindler

What are you doing for a living?

Pippa Pegg Now
I work as a Cif Resistor

And what are you doing for a living

???

I work as a Tiffin Regulator from the 1990's

What you do for a living?

I work as a Vigilante Officer for Shepherds

Okay so tell me what you do for a living

I work as a Translator for a Vol au Vent

So tell me what's your profession ?

I work as a Demure Pasty Analyser

What do you do for living ??

I work as a Hologram Supplier for Mezzanines

What do you do for a living?

I work as a Raisin Influencer for Aquafresh

## MORE SILLY STUFF

The following conversations don't really fall into a particular category, largely because the scammer doesn't even get that far. Sometimes it's good to get the scammer on the back foot. It's amazing where it can lead.

## MANDY CIRCLES AND BILL THE FISH

Sometimes, you get a message from an old friend and the memories just come flooding back. Here was I, minding my own business, when I get a DM from my old mucker Mark Luis. I could not believe it! Neither could he to be fair...

 Hello

Mark Luis? Is that you??!!

 Yes.

Oh my god!! After all these years.. I can't believe it!! It must be 25 years since we last spoke.

I just could not believe it – it was Mark Luis from school. For those who don't know, Mark and I used to be the best friends in school. We would sit next to each other in Maths. We would copy each other's science homework. It was the absolute best of times. But then life gets in the way, and you just lose contact with each other.

That was until now.

Mark and I had had such a lot to catch up on. Probably more that he was expecting to be honest...

Wow!! I just can't believe it!! I'm good thanks. Really good. Where do I start? I started my own business, did really well... became a millionaire! I know right, me, a millionaire? Ridiculous

Clearly it was great that Mark and I were catching up – as the kids say – 'it had been time'. It was really to speak to Mark – we had clearly missed each other's company. To be honest, it was a bit of relief to hear Mark's voice. Because there had been rumours...

Hey there was a rumour going around you were dead! Can you believe that??!

 Seriously I'm alive honey

Well, that's laid those rumours to rest. Mark was alive and well.

Wow!! I can't believe it... so fill me in on the last 25 years or so! What's going on in your life?

Mark was not only alive and well, but prone to giving the occasional dodgy answer to a simple question.

Wow this world is really sphere

 Thank God. I'm doing great and you?

'Wow. This world is really sphere'. Love that answer. I think in the translation it was supposed to be 'It's a small world' so I will give our scammer a 6/10 for

effort. I told Mark Luis that things were going well for me. I had started my own business.

 What kind of business

Yeah I started up a business called 'Lemons on a Hill'. I sold lemons on top of this hill. It was fine. Just fine.

Mark Luis said that after school, he got a job and is now part of the military. A scammer telling me they have a job in the military? Say it ain't so!

Military? Really? Wow' we used to call you Luis the Loser...

Yeah.
Luis the Loser hahaha

 Tell me are you married?

So, Mark and I were getting on pretty well. It had been lovely to catch up with him. He was certainly the same kind of guy I remembered from school, that cheeky monkey with a silly grin. But it seemed in the last 25 years, Mark has certainly grown up. I explained to Mark that I wasn't married. I was currently single and without children. He seemed to like that. I know, strange, right? But I didn't want to talk about me, I wanted to talk about the old times.

Do you remember the old crew??

Remember KettleFish Freddie?

Replied to you

Remember KettleFish Freddie?

Wow yeah yeah 😆

Oh no. This was going to break his heart. Sit down for this news.

He's dead

Really

He got hit by a van full of treacle

Awful times

Sadly, KettleFish Freddie wasn't the first of our school alumni to have passed on.

Remember Bill the Fish?

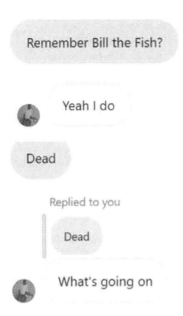
Yeah I do

Dead

Replied to you

Dead

What's going on

Yes, I can imagine for Mark this weas a pretty traumatic way to find out this awful news. Sadly, the bad news kept coming.

He drowned in a bucket of raisins

100

Despite learning about the death of both KettleFish Freddie and Bill the Fish, it seemed that Mark had got over the grief pretty quickly as his next message came a bit out of the blue.

Baby you're looking good

Beautiful

---

100 Swept away by the currant.

Grief can do many things to many different people. Typically with grief, you may express one or more of these emotions: Guilt, anger, irritability, rage, despair, regret, anxiety, loneliness, denial, yearning, sadness, worry, isolation, self-pity, envy, fear and hopelessness. In this instance, grief just made Mark horny.

> baby I'm interested in you, I'm serious this time, not joking.

Wow! I wasn't expecting this[101]. It turns out that Mark had feelings for me. After all these years, Mark Luis from school was telling me he was interested in me. And this time, he was serious. The problem was that Mark and I had had a bit of a moment 25 years ago when we were back in school. I wondered if he remembered.

> You broke my heart last time. Remember?

> You got off with Debbie Bunsen in front of me

Mark appeared to have been a changed man. Yes, he looked different. Really different. But he was a more mature person now. So, maybe he wouldn't make the same mistakes that I remember for him for.

> Replied to you
>
> > You got off with Debbie Bunsen in front of me

> I'm sorry, really hurting I'm sorry, please forgive me 😩

As a way of persuading that I was the one, he also sent me a photo of himself

---

[101] I was.

looking very coquettish.

It was clear that Mark had changed and as we exchanged more and more messages, it appeared that we were getting closer and closer. Although, to be honest, he did look a lot different to how (I had imagined) he looked in school 25 years ago.

> Just looking at some old school photos

> You look so different

> Replied to you
>
> > You look so different

>  That's life baby, time brings change

'Time brings change'. I was really starting to like this guy again. I loved this proverb.

> Did you get an A-Level in Wise??

Mark and I chatted about his family and his work. He explained that he was single, he had a child from a previous relationship and his wife had died 4 years ago. Since then, he was looking to seek a new relationship with someone... and then I popped back into his life. Well, technically he messaged me first – but you get the idea.

I wondered what Mark wanted. Was it help organising a special school reunion? Was it to relay a message to his parents? I kept wondering what it possibly could be. What do you think it could possibly be, reader?

> Please get me an ITunes card,
> really can't go out now to get it

Oh, right. Mark wanted a $200 iTunes card because he was in the barracks and couldn't not get one himself. I wonder why he wanted a $200 iTunes card? The Belinda Carlisle back catalogue? All of the good Foo Fighters albums from the last 20 years? I wonder what'd he'll do with the remaining $200[102].

I said to Mark that I would think about, but in the meantime, I was a little bit busy seeing an old friend.

---

[102] Zing. But, seriously, name a decent Foo Fighters album in the last 20 years?

> I'm seeing Mandy Circles for breakfast this morning. Remember her from school? We're still close friends so I'll mention I'm back in contact with you...

We talk later ♥, don't forget to get the card I'm waiting please.

I was all set to enjoy a lovely breakfast with Mandy Circles, when I was hit with some of the biggest and most disturbing news I had ever heard.

OH MY GODDDDDDDDDDD!!!

 What's wrong

Something was going on, and I needed to confront Mark Luis about it.

> I'm here with Mandy. She just told me that Mark Luis died in a fishing accident in 2014!

WHO ARE YOU?????

I had to confront Mark about this! What would he say? Who was he?! What the ruddy heck was going on? Was I being conned? Scammed?

Replied to you

> Mandy is here. She just told me
> that Mark Luis from school died
> in a fishing accident in 2014.

 That fake news about me.

Fake news? Alright Donald, calm down! I need to get more information from
Mark, but I had even more information from Mandy Circles to give Mark.

SHE WENT TO YOUR FUNERAL!

I wanted to know what Mark thought about this revelation. I needed to get to
the bottom of what the ruddy heck was going on. It seemed to me that
something was slightly off about Mark Luis – but I couldn't quite put my finger
on it.

Replied to you

> SHE WENT TO YOUR FUNERAL!

 She's not sure

Was my trusted friend Mandy Circles telling the truth? Was Mark Luis telling
the truth? Someone had to be telling the truth[103]. I had to find the truth. Like
Mulder and Scully, the truth was out there. I asked Mark a question that he
really should know the answer to.

---

[103] Spoiler alert: no-one was.

I'm alive

What are your parents names?

 Why asking me such questions, you mean I don't know them

Fan stop asking such questions

Why did he not know the names of his parents? Why was he not willing to share this information? What was going on?

 I can't remember anything about them right now. Things really fall apart ♥

You know how it goes. You can easily remember your old school friends from 25 years ago, Mandy Circles, Debbie Bunsen and KettleFish Freddie, but you don't remember the names of your parents?

Just to confirm, you don't remember your parents names?

But yet you remember me from 25 years ago

The game was up for Mark Luis sadly. He knew he was rumbled.

He blocked me, and we both moved on. He moved on to his next victim, and I moved on and continued my fictious breakfast[104] with Mandy Circles.

---

[104] 2 x sausage, 2 x bacon, 1 x hash brown, 1 x mushrooms, 1 x baked beans.

## BREXIT

Oh Brexit, you complex bastard. Before the big vote of 2016, there was a lot of information and disinformation being thrown at us Brits, telling us the why we should remain or leave the EU. Thankfully, when presented with facts, the British people know what to do. And when a fact such as saving £350m a week which would be spent on the NHS, we went and voted with our baked bean covered fingers and ticked the box that would indeed bring zero benefits and nothing but hardship, red tape and division for decades to come. But at least we don't have to eat bendy bananas.

However, it isn't just Britons that know about Brexit. Our Nigerian scammer friends also know about it too. Well, our Nigerian scammer friends dressed up as hot sexy dudes, pretending to be hot sexy dudes.

Anyway, me and 'Random Instagram Follower 1003'[105] were getting on like a house on fire. He mentioned that he lived in Ireland. When I pressed him, whereabouts in Ireland he lived, he was a little vague.

 Island in Europe ok

'Island (sic) in Europe' OK?! I pressed again. Whereabouts in Ireland, you lying toad? 'Random Instagram Follower 1003' said they lived in the beautiful city of Cork, Ireland's second biggest city. Although after a recent visit there, you cannot for love nor money get a taxi to the airport from the city centre in the middle of the day. Ireland's second biggest city indeed.

After claiming I have family in Cork (I don't) I asked them whereabouts in Cork they're from. This is the problem with scammers. They're not great at thinking on their feet. And so, when you ask someone 'Whereabouts in Cork do you live'? – instead of looking at Cork on Google Maps and picking out a random place, they reply with this:

 Weather: 9°C, Wind W at 37 km/h, 76% Humidity

Thanks Michael Fish for the weather update. But there was more.

---

[105] Not the real username.

Area: 187 km²

And of course:

 Local time: Wednesday 21:54

I was starting to get a little bit sceptical of 'Random Instagram Follower 1003'? The more he messaged me, the more my suspicions were aroused.

 Population: 124,391 (2016)
United Nations

Well, it seemed that I was dealing with a very intelligent person. I mean, if you can recall the population of Cork from the 2016 census off the top of your head – then we are dealing with a boffin of the highest order. With that in mind, I wanted to get more information from him. Maybe I could learn something from him. So, I asked him what his view on Brexit was...

What's your view on Brexit?

 I thought the UK had already left the EU

I could tell that 'Random Instagram Follower 1003'was a very wise and intelligent man and he continued the conversation. With himself.

It has. The UK voted to leave the EU in 2016 and officially left the trading bloc - its nearest and biggest trading partner - on 31 January 2020

He continued again. With himself.

> However, both sides agreed to
> keep many things the same until
> 31 December 2020, to allow
> enough time to agree to the
> terms of a new trade deal.

> It was a complex, sometimes
> bitter negotiation, but they
> finally agreed a deal on 24
> December

It was indeed a complex and sometimes bitter negotiation. But, finally on 24 December 2021, we got over the line, and it's been ~~an absolute shitstorm~~ plain sailing ever since. Without wanting, asking or requesting any more information, 'Instagram Follower 1,003' continued with his knowledge of the UK's exiting from the European Union.

> The UK has voted to leave the
> EU by 52% to 48%. Leave won
> the majority of votes in England
> and Wales, while every council in
> Scotland saw Remain majorities

At this point I wondered if 'Random Instagram Follower 1003' was Lord David Frost (Europe Advisor to the Prime Minister and Chief Negotiator), Steve Barclay (Secretary of State for Exiting the European Union) or Sir Tim Barrow (UK Permanent Representative to the EU). As I was dealing with an EU expert, I thought I would get down and ask him more about some of the characters that were part of the Brexit process.

> Do you trust Nigel Farage?

No

I had to find out who 'Random Instagram Follower 1003' was. I knew that this person didn't trust Nigel Farage, but that's the equivalent of asking the question 'Have they got a bucket on their head?' on the first round of Guess Who.

> Why don't you trust Nigel Farage?

Is not a good man

Oh, come on... Old Nigel? Don't barrage the Farage! He continued...

> Nigel Paul Farage is a British broadcaster and former politician who was Leader of the UK Independence Party from 2006 to 2009 and 2010 to 2016 and Leader of the Brexit Party from 2019 to 2021.

It looked like someone was looking at the Nigel Paul Farage Wikipedia page. So, I had a quick look at the site too. Here's a few facts about Nigel Paul Farage that I didn't know.

- He was named 'Briton of the Year' by The Times in 2014.
- His father was called Guy Justus Oscar Farage.
- He likes to relax by fishing alone at night on the Kent coast.

It was at this point that I actually thought that I wasn't dealing with a Nigerian scammer at all, but someone even worse than that. I thought I was talking to the actual Nigel Farage. Suddenly terrified that his right-wing views might encroach through my body like 'Instagram Osmosis'[106] like what had happened to 75% of my grandparents, I decided to block 'Random Instagram Follower 1003' as quickly as possible and head to church for forgiveness.

---

[106] Instagram Osmosis: The name of the upcoming Radiohead album.

**UNDERCOVER BOSS**

I got a lovely message from good friend Adeleke Adeniuga. I don't know Adeleke but I followed back and she started messaging me. Adeleke and I went back and forth on a number of issues – and then she started calling me on Instagram, demanding that I pick up the phone. Erm, oh heck. I had to think up an excuse as to why I couldn't pick up the phone...

> If my boss sees me he will hit me

> You're mad

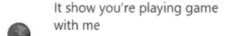

> It show you're playing game with me

> You don't know Tony Rossiter I presume

Tony Rossiter is of course a name I have made up as my boss for this conversation. Tony Rossiter is one of my favourites made up names. Fun fact, the name Dave Rossiter comes up in the Das Ingtons song 'Algorithm'[107].

*'Your name is Dave Rossiter,*
*And you are unfamiliar.*
*I've never heard of you.*
*Judging by your avatar, we don't look very similar,*
*but I am happy to discover people new...'*

So, anyway in this scenario, we are painting the picture that I cannot pick up his phone call because my boss Tony Rossiter has major anger issues and would resort to violence should he see me on the phone. I kept telling Adeleke that Tony was such an unreasonable boss.

---

[107] Google it Grandad, it's an absolute hit!

My job is so bad. They make us wear bags and we have to piss into bags and keep working.

That's suck

What the fuck

I kept talking about how much of a bad man Tony Rossiter was. I told Adeleke that Tony once had us work late. Until 6pm. That's how much of a tyrant he was. That and the killing of people with his bare hands.

Tony Rossiter is a bad bad man

And he is my boss

 So???

And he killed my best friend

With his hands

I keep telling you Adeleke, my boss Tony Rossiter would kill me if I picked up the call from you. Just like he killed my best friend with his hands. His bare hands. His naked bare hands. How will Adeleke respond?

Don't talk to me again if you
can't do what I asked you to do

rn

Are you Tony Rossiter?

Yes

Huge development. For those late to the party, this is where we are. We have a Nigerian scammer with a fake profile called Adeleke, who is now pretending to be called Tony Rossiter, who is the boss of Pippa, a fake profile account created by someone called James. There are so many levels to this – it really makes The Godfather seems like Gogglebox. So, as it turned out, I was talking to my boss – and as such, I thought I better ask a few questions.

Hello Tony

Can I get paid early this month?

Oh and about the canteen area,
we need more decaf coffee
please

And we're running out of Rich
Tea biscuits

Eventually the scammer got bored. Bored of speaking to me.

Look, we have employee rules for a reason. You can't just say 'Pls get lost' to one of your employees. It's not 1988 or Taggart anymore. Yes, back in the day I could call DI Burnside a 'bent bastard' to his face, but times have changed.

As an employee at Fictional Organisation PLC, I demand that Tony Rossiter/Adeleke Adenuga apologise for the outburst and also respond to latest employee request.

It seemed that Tony wasn't concerned about employee wellbeing. Typical, it seemed Fictional Org PLC was all about the mighty dollar and cared little about their employees. I asked myself why I continued to work at Fictional Org PLC. There was only reason why I worked at Fictional Org PLC. It has and has always been Tony. I couldn't lie to myself any longer. I had feelings for Tony, and I had to tell him.

I think I love you

I don't wanna see your texts anymore ok

Yes, Tony is my boss. But you just can't choose who you love with. I will not apologise for this. I am sorry Tony Rossiter. All these years of working together at Fictional Org PLC, my feelings, my heart, my desires...

After this revelation, Tony/Adeleke did the only thing to stop. He blocked me. Which is a shame. As I really liked him pretending to be a boss in a fictional company. I miss you Adeleke. I miss you. As the kids say, 'call me bbe'. But not on Friday obvs, as I'm not working.

**ACHTUNG – HOSTAGE!**

manuelfrancois27    Message    ✓≗    ⌄    •••

2 posts    56 followers    107 following

**Manuel Francois**
Study

The next scammer goes by the name Manuel Francois. Her profile is her looking coquettish whilst wearing some headphones. I wonder what she's listening to. I'd like to think it's the Brazilian death metal band, Sepultura and their excellent 1993 album Chaos AD. Alas, we will never know. Manuel followed me, I followed back. She messaged me instantly. It's a story as old as time.

> How was your family and your
> wife and your kids

What? What did she know about my family?!?

> You've got my wife and kids
> hostage?

> Please release them!!

Always get them on the back foot. Always.

> What did you mean and what
> are you talking about ?

Clearly, Manuel was unaware that my entire family (including dog) were taken hostage last year by an evil group of evil people. They had evilly[108] done evil

---

[108] Didn't think that was a word. Turns out it was.

things and had their evil wicked ways with my non-evil family.

> My wife and kids were taken
> hostage last year

> And you ask how they are

> You have taken them hostage

> Release my family!

> Are they alive?

 Yes

OMG Manuel Francois! You dirty devil. Like, WTF you know! Holy hijack situation. Straight away, the scammer had gone from messaging a potential victim, to being embroiled in a fake kidnapping. Obvs I was heartbroken that my family and dog had been kidnapped, but I was so grateful to know that they were still alive after all this time. They were still with us.

> Please I beg of you. Please send
> a photo of my little boy, Reggie
> Seldom. I need to see him

How would the hijacker respond? What is it that hijackers normally demand? What is it that scammers want? I think we had the same answer...

 Not yet until you pay for him
okay

I bloody knew it. As quick as a flash, the scammer had spotted an opportunity to get some cash out of this. Now, we know from the movies that kidnapped people mean large sums of money being demanded. However, for the purposes of this book, I went onto the internet and asked Jeeves what the average ransom was for a kidnapping in the real world. Have a quick guess in your head as to what you think it is. Ok, take that number, double it. You with me so far? Now add six, divide it in half, and subtract the number you started with. Is the answer three?[109]

Anyhow, I did a bit of Googling and found the average ransom kidnap demand in 2021 was $368,901, up 42% from 2018 – literally the definition of the cost-of-living crisis. So, let's see what Manuel Francois was charging to give my beloved family back to me.

Just go to any nearby store to you and get a Razer card of $2000 to release your family to you okay

110

$2,000 doesn't seem a lot – probably cost the kidnappers at least that in food at least. Nevertheless, I really wanted to see my fake family again so I messaged back saying I would pay the ransom.

I asked if my wife, my daughter, my son and my dog were all alive. After having confirmation of this, I got the kidnappers instructions.

---

[109] Spooky.
[110] Razer card is a card for gamer and one of the most popular gift cards in Nigeria.

Quickly get the card right now
so we can release your family

Your son is asking for you

And he said his name is Reggie
seldom

 Or Apple gift card or steam okay

I liked that the kidnappers were giving me payment options – first it was a Razer card, now it was an Apple gift card or a steam card. Naturally I asked if the kidnappers accepted Klarna. Shop now, pay later. Plus, it means I can return them if I don't like them.

Please! My darling boy Reggie

How is he? I've not seen him in such a long time

Manuel Francois confirmed they were all still alive. She confirmed that nothing would go wrong if I made the payment and made the payment fast.

Please don't hurt my family

 Make sure you get it after you finish work okay

I almost updated my Facebook status with this – 'That moment when your kidnapped family are about to be released, but you got to get that report to Wendy from Accounts by 4pm #FML #YOLO #WendyFromAccounts'.
The plan was simple. As soon as Manuel Francois had the card, she would

release my family.

I we tell them to relax okay so
once you get the card I we
release them to you okay

It seemed to be an easy transaction. Nothing could go wrong. Or could it? I finished 'fake' work and headed back to my 'fake' home so I could focus on getting the steam card and getting my 'fake' family back. Just when you thought everything was going swimmingly, you wouldn't believe what happened next.

OH MY GOD

What happened

MY FAMILY HAVE JUST WALKED THROUGH THE DOOR!!! THEY ARE BACK!

Can you believe it? On the very day I was going to pay $2,000 for their release, my wonderful family (and dog) come bounding through the front door.

It was an incredible reunion. So, we all went out to a Wimpy to eat burgers with a knife and fork using the $2,000 steam card as payment.

After realising the game was up, and I was taking him for a ride, he just sent me a quick message before blocking me.

Guy you fuck up

**STREWTH!**

This is Eric. Eric is a military man. Eric started following me out of nowhere. I followed him back, because I am nice like that. Eric and I were talking about all sorts of things. He told me he was a fitness man and likes to run. I asked Eric what his 5K personal best was. This was his response.

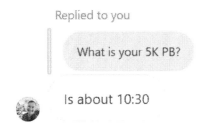

10 minutes and 30 seconds? For 5K? Now folks, when I am not writing a book on silly scammers and not working a normal job, I like to put on the running shoes and pound the pavements. I've done plenty of 5Ks in the past[111]. But 10:30 for 5,000m? What the ruddy heckers? I asked him if he was sure. He said he was adamant that this was his personal best for 5K.

I did advise that it's possible that he may have been lying to me and proceeded to show him the world record for 5,000m which would mean he would have beaten that time by nearly two minutes.

---

[111] PB is 23:35 for anyone asking.

# 5000 metres world record progression

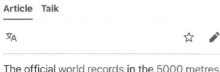

The official world records in the 5000 metres are held by Joshua Cheptegei with 12:35.36 for men and Letesenbet Gidey with 14:06.62 for women.

That didn't seem to faze Eric.

> We run during our training

> Though I don't normally take record of it

 But I think I'm very fast

I love Eric's vibe. 'Yeah, chill out guys. I'm not really runner – but I normally beat the world record for 5K by about two minutes. No biggie guys. No biggie'. Eric and I were beginning to become friends, and he asked me what the origin of name Pippa was.

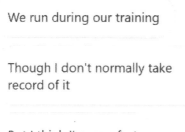

It is a name my mother gave me. She said she is reminded of Pippa from Home and Away, and that she wanted to live in Summer Hay at the time and know Donald Fisher

Eric seemed interested in Donald Fisher. Very interested in Donald Fisher.

256

Is Donald Fisher died?

Donald Fisher is alive.

But he's wanted by Alf and Morag as he was given money by them to visit Marilyn in England

Take yourself back to Summer Bay in the late 1990's. Are you ready?

My mother wrote a poem for Donald

Do you want to hear it?

Eric was all in. He knew that my mother was in love with Donald Fisher.

 Yes Pippa I'd love to hear it

Here we go. Prepare yourself.

> You know we belong together
> You and I forever and ever
> No matter where you are
> You're my guiding star
> And from the very first moment
> I saw you
> I never felt such emotion
> (oooooh)
> I'm walking on air
> Just to know...(just to know)
> You are there...(you are there)
>
> Hold me in your arms
> don't let me go
> I want to stay forever
> home and away
> with you each day
>
> Let me be the one that you turn
> to
> Someone you can rely on
> Closer each day
> Home and away

I'm really pleased with this poem that I definitely wrote. I hope that Eric liked it too.

> Though I can't get the actual
> tune for it but reading it alone is
> very emotional

 She really got much love for
Donald Fisher

I had to fill Eric in on the backstory of Donald Fisher. To do this I had to Wikipedia 'Donald Fisher'[112]. I told Eric the story of Donald Fisher through the wonderful words of Wikipedia.

---

[112] I'm 44 years old.

His son Alan died of a brain aneurysm. When this happened Donald Fisher changed his ways. He and Bobby developed a warm friendship and he became more fair and relaxed... even though he was sometimes still grumpy

Eric said he really enjoyed the story and asked more about Donald Fisher.

 Do you like what he did ?

He was a firm but fair headmaster at Summer Bay High School

Eric said he really wanting to have a relationship with me. It seemed my stories about Donald Fisher and the Summer Bay shenanigans had really made Eric fall in love with me. He told me all about himself. He said he liked cooking. He said he liked reading. He told me he liked blues music. I asked him why any sane person would listen to blues music, and he responded with this.

Blues

I love it so much

It makes me emotional

 And think real deep

I often think about Eric. Well, I often think about Eric thinking real deep about blues music. Sadly, this is where the story ends between me and Eric. He was

too deep into blues music for us to work out. Oh, and he was a Nigerian scammer. I often forget that bit.

## VOODOO / SPIRITUAL READING

Not all dodgy Instagram accounts want to find true love. Scammers will use all sorts of different tactics to get money from you. Another method is contacting Instagram users and asking if they want a spiritual reading. Now, I told you earlier that scammers like to target vulnerable people. Just like Sally Morgan, scammers love to get vulnerable people to part with their money. Let's have a look at some psychic advisor scams.

## HARRY POTTER AND THE BERKSHIRE TOWN

Hello xx

Hi angel sorry to bother you! I am a God gifted Psychic Advisor & Love Specialist. I'm drawn to you I would love to have the opportunity to read for you and and spiritual guidance, healing, meditation and other spiritual works if you're interested let me know! Thank you God bless 🖤 🖤💜

A God gifted psychic advisor and love specialist! In the Venn diagram of two such matters, you'd think there wouldn't be much crossover, but you live and learn! A cross between Derek Acorah and Cilla Black. And, Surprise, Surprise I replied back to them. I advised them that I was very much interested in the reading, but it probably wasn't the normal kind of reading they had in mind. Instead of a love or spiritual reading, I wanted the self-titled 'God gifted Psychic Advisor and Love Specialist' to read me chapters of a Harry Potter book.

Great. How much to read 'Harry Potter' to me?

Slightly taken back, and possibly not quite understand my request, the GGPAALS[113] replied they would for the price of $30, read me some chapters of

Harry Potter. Which of the Harry Potter books should they read to me? 'Harry Potter and The Waste of Everyone's Time', 'Harry Potter and The Man in The Pointy Hat' or 'Harry Potter and You're 33 Sarah, Shouldn't You Be Reading Adult Books?'. Regardless, let's find out more from Scammy Potter[114].

> How many chapters will that be?

> It will be like 5

> If you ready are you using cashapp or PayPal??

A deal was made with the scammer, and they were going to read 5 chapters of 'Harry Potter and The Tuna and Sweetcorn Jacket Potato' to me. Our God gifted Psychic Advisor and Love Specialist asked for payment via PayPal and gave their email address.

> Marymilikau@outlook.com

> Ok. Gonna sign you up to the Razorlight mailing list

So – this is what I did. I signed our friendly scammer to the actual Razorlight mailing list for the radio friendly 00's indie band so they can be updated on all things Razorlight. I also sent them a link to Razorlight playing their hit 'America' live on CD:UK. Fun fact: Despite reaching #1 in the UK and number 29 in The Swiss Hit Parade, the song 'America' was never actually released in America. I waited a few minutes for the scammer to listen to the song and tried to get some feedback.

---

[113] God gifted Psychic Advisor and Love Specialist.
[114] You're welcome.

What did you think of them?

Ok

In terms of music reviews, it's not really the New Musical Express, is it? I like my music reviews to fall slightly in the middle between the overly long hyperbolic drivel the NME puts out and the one word review our scammer gave. To be fair though, I had much respect for our scammer on this. Because I myself used to do music reviews. Very short music reviews. I could review an artist's album in simply two words. Don't believe me? Here's a two-word review of Michael Jackson's Thriller album[115].

Anyway, I next sent the lyrics to Razorlight's biggest hit.

All my life
Watching America
All my life
There's panic in America
Oh oh oh, oh
There's trouble in America
Oh oh oh, oh

Here's a quick aside: Have a quick guess as to how many streams of 'America' there have been on Spotify? Yeah, double it and add a few million[116].

Alas, our conversation moved on from Razorlight and more important matters – the Harry Potter reading. But I am not sure if it was a language or culture barrier, but things took a slightly odd turn.

---

[115] Not 'Bad'.
[116] 129 million.

> Am want to do reading for you

> Do you mean Reading?

> Yes

> Oh great. That's good. I'm up for a tour of Reading. What does it involve?

This is why you should meet new people. One day you are signing someone up to the mailing list to Razorlight, and within seconds you have arranged to do a tour of a large market town in Berkshire.

We went back and forth – while I was trying to arrange a reading of a Harry Potter book whilst on a bus tour in the town of Reading, the scammer was trying their hardest to steer the conversation back to getting $30 paid into their PayPal account. I then decided to change tactics and swapped the reading of the Harry Potter novel for another book.

> Will you read me my favourite book, Scamming On Instagram Just Won't Work by Ivor Nomorals?

And then they blocked me...

Fun fact: I am also signed up to the Razorlight mailing list – and as a result get twice monthly emails from the Razorlight mailing list. Even though there really isn't any Razorlight news and there hasn't been any Razorlight news since about 2005.

Genuinely, I have tried to unsubscribe from the Razorlight mailing list, on many many occasions, but try as I might, every couple of weeks another email comes through from Razorlight telling me what the band are up to (not a lot) and where you can listen to their music (the usual places).

I sometimes wonder if this is the scammers ultimate revenge... Yeah, that

James Billington, he may waste our time, he may waste our phone data – but forever he will be subscribed to the Razorlight mailing list until the day he dies, with him being told what the band are up to (not a lot) and how you can listen to their music (the usual places).

## SPELLCASTING: ENLARGEMENT

Here's me minding my own business, sitting on the couch, contemplating my life. When suddenly, I get a message that could change my life forever. I reached into my pocket and took out my phone. It was a message on Instagram. As I looked at the words, I realised that this was the message I had been for all my life.

Friday June 24, 2022. 5:30pm. The date. The time. It will go down in history. The message was from a spell caster, and they were telling me that they could better my life through the mysterious power of spells.

> Hello lovely 🦋 🖤, I'm am a
> Spell caster, I am here to put a
> new page of happiness in your
> life, The following are spells I'm
> specialized in and be rest
> assured I can help you with any:
>
> * Tarot/life Reading
> * * Ex back spell
> * love /Obsession spell
> * * money spell
> * lottery spell
> * * weight loss/gain spell
> * enlargement spell for body
> parts (hips,boobs,ass,d*ck)
> * * protection spell
> * pregnancy spell for barren
> * * Bad energy Removal
> * cleansing spell/
> Note: my spells has no side
> effects and it is 100%
> guaranteed to work. Pick a spell
> of interest for more info dm me
> via WhatsApp

Wow! I could choose any spell I like. Please do remember reader that the spells have no side effects and are 100% guaranteed, so you know you are dealing with some real authentic shit. Forget getting on a Ryanair plane to Bodrum for a new set of teeth – this is the real deal! What would I choose? Bigger hips? Weight gain? Obsession spell? Pregnancy spell for the barren[117]?

I went for a sit-down wee to contemplate. After a shake and wipe, I decided there was only one thing I was interested in...

> Can I choose d*ck enlargement please

Yeah, I know reader. You bloody shallow person, James. There's more to life than having a bigger d*ick. But I thought this was important. It's important for confidence issues. It's important for my self-esteem and it's important for... look, it's just important, OK?!

> Can you make my d*ck bigger?

Yes of course

Have done that too so meany people who ask for it

This was great news. The spell caster has done it to 'meany' people (wondering if that means 'Nasty' Nick from Big Brother and Piers Morgan?) so it looks like it's going to be good. Remember this is 100% guaranteed. The next part was going to be a bit more uncomfortable. I had to send a picture of my d*ck to the spell caster, so they knew what they were dealing with. I didn't really want to put a picture of my d*ck in this book – but I feels it's important to be open and transparent. You've not spent £10[118] to be short-changed.

After agreeing with the spell caster that I needed to send him a picture of my d*ick before we talk about payment, it was time.

---

[117] Good name for a band.
[118] ish

After much deliberation, I sent the scammer a picture of my tiny d*ck.

He blocked both me and my tiny d*ck.

## ONLINE VOTING

Have you ever been contacted by a stranger asking for you to vote for them to in an online ambassador program? No, of course you haven't! But I have on many occasions.

> Hey I'm contesting for an
> ambassadorship spot at an
> online influencer program
> please can you vote for me

The 'online voting' scam is quite innovative. You'll get a message from a scammer asking to vote for them in some sort of contest. The details are scarce. No information on what the contest is. No details on what they win. No details on the company running the contest. No real information on why they are contacting strangers to get them to vote in this contest! However, they're not asking for money, so it's all legit, right? Of course not!

The scammer will tell you all they need is for you to vote for them. There's not a link which takes you to a voting form online. All they ask is that you put their email address in the 'personal details' of your Instagram account and then send them a screenshot. What an easy (and very unconventional) way to vote for something. I'll be honest, it's not how I voted for One True Voice to win X-Factor back in the day. Once you have changed your email address in your Instagram personal details and sent them a screenshot, the scammer will attempt to log into your account on Instagram. They will click 'forgot password' and the password reset email will then go to their email address. The scammer can then change the password and have access to your account, and there's not a lot you can do about it. In fact, only 30% of users can recover their account after an Instagram hacking.

Once a scammer has access to your account, they can edit that account to their content and there's very little you can do about it. Hackers will post as you on your account and encourage your followers to invest in bitcoin and other types of cryptocurrencies. Of course, as discussed before, there's no actual investment, only a scam that swindles money from your unsuspecting friends and family members.

**THROWING ENOUGH SHIT AT A WALL**

volker.paul.3    Message    ✓🔾    • • •

0 posts    1,410 followers    4,024 following

**Anna Volker Paul**

Followed by jennycarson582

This is Volker.paul.3 aka Anna. Despite sounding like a test name for a rocket, Anna was one of my favourites. You can tell straight away that this is a scam account. How on earth do you manage to accumulate 1,410 followers despite not posting any pictures? They are following lots more people that they have followers, and they call themselves Anna despite having an impressive full beard. After following me, Anna sent me a message and straight away went for the ambassador scam.

Hey I'm contesting for an ambassadorship spot at an online influencer program please can you vote for me

Despite us not knowing each other, Anna was obviously keen to win the ambassador spot and I have no doubt he was messaging all his followers. I was more than happy to go along with the 'ambassador scam' and would do what I could to make sure that Anna won!

I'll send you an entry link via sms messages immediately you get it take a screenshot of the link and send it back to me don't click it

In these scenarios, the scammer will try to log into your account, and request a password reset. Depending on what security you have set up with Instagram, usually Instagram will send you a password request email and that's what 'Anna' is wanting here. Once you have a password request, they want you to put their email address into your personal information. They'll ask for a screenshot confirming you have done this, and then when they request a password reset on your account – hey presto, it will go to their email. They can then set the password to whatever they like, and more importantly will have access to your account.

Sadly, this didn't quite work for Anna in the way he/she wanted.

> Add your number to your personal information on your profile done Instagram Will verify you now

Despite sending many messages on how to do this very simple task, it seemed that I wasn't quite understanding. As a result, Anna got more and more frustrated. Anna was hoping that I would be receiving an email from Instagram asking me to reset my password. I did receive an email. Sadly, for Anna, it wasn't from Instagram.

> I've just received an email

> Take a screenshot of the email let me see if is the correct email

> It's from my local greengrocer saying they've got an offer on lemons

> Its 3 for 2 on lemons

Clearly, this confused Anna. Here he was, looking to gain access to my Instagram account, and here is me, quite rightly, telling him about this incredible offer from my local greengrocers.

Send a screenshot of the message you got there

From my local greengrocers?

Ok

Now I didn't obviously have an email from my greengrocers about lemons. I didn't have an email from my greengrocers at all. I didn't even know any greengrocers. I'm not even a huge fan of vegetables. Although I really like mange tout[119]. Despite this, the closest I got to knowing a greengrocer, was my dad who used to work at the deli counter in a supermarket. He got sacked for his poor customer service. He kept giving everyone the cold shoulder[120].

Despite telling these jokes that went over the scammers head, I ploughed on. I crafted a generic lemon-based offer email on the Notes function on my phone and screenshotted it over to Anna.

### When life gives you lemons!

You know we're lemon crazy here at Greengrocers R' Us, and as we head into the weekend we wanted to tell you the big news!

We're giving you an offer that's too good to be true! That's right, for a limited time period – we're offering a deal of 3 for 2 on lemons. That's right, you buy 2 lemons and get your $3^{rd}$ lemon absolutely free.

The lemon offer won't lemon last long and lemon will be removed lemon an any time lemon we see fit.

So come down now to Greengrocers R' Us for a great lemon deal – as we say here 'Fruit and Veg. It's the best. We love Fruit and Veg.'

Best regards

Barry and Julie

---

[119] Mange Tout is my favourite movie sequel. I can't wait for Mange Three.
[120] Sorry.

I thought Anna would be interested in this fantastic, once in a lifetime deal. Even scammers need Vitamin C[121].

Do you want any lemons?

 I don't think so for now

Its 3 for 2 though

(Just on lemons)

What would happen? Would Anna be tempted by the offer on lemons? Would Anna be tempted by anything else from Greengrocers R'Us? Barry and Julie are obviously trying to tempt customers into their store for the lemon offer, and hope customers pick up some more great perishable bargains. This could include mushrooms. This could include courgettes. You get the idea. Let's see what Anna says.

 Actually I'm a senior account manager in bitcoin mining ,have you heard about Bitcoin before?

You have to respect the scammer here. He started with the 'ambassador' scam and is now pivoting over to the bitcoin mining scam. He's doing his best to do anything he can to try to lure me into giving him money. I, however, wasn't about to let a deal as good as this (3 for 2 on lemons) pass anyone by.

---

[121] 'Even scammers need Vitamin C' should have been the title of this book.

I'm gonna take advantage

You can put slices of lemon in water..

We were at a stalemate. It was Bitcoins vs lemons[122] which also sounds like it could be the final in The Hundred cricket competition. Who would win this epic contest?

 Actually I'm a senior account manager in bitcoin mining ,have you heard about Bitcoin before?

Yeah you've said this

I'm talking about lemons

And this amazing lemon offer

I was adamant that I was not going to let Anna miss out on this deal. It was 3 for 2 on lemons. You don't miss out on this once in a lifetime opportunity.

---

[122] 'Bitcoins vs Lemons' should have been the title of this book.

I tell you what

Send me your address and I'll
send you 3 lemons in the post

I do not need lemon

Did you know you buy 2 lemons
and get a 3rd lemon absolutely
free!

It was at this point where Anna asked me for a steam card. If you are playing a game of 'Scammer Bingo' this guy is shouting 'House'. In the end, I broke the fourth wall, and I told 'Anna' how impressed I was with his doggedness in looking to try and scam me.

I like that you started off with
the online voting scam first, and
when that didn't work, you went
to the Bitcoin scam.. and now
you're just like 'give me a
bloody steam card'

Classic!

How would 'Anna' react to the fact that I was onto him, and knew he was trying a number of ways to scam me?

Opss

I wasn't the one that sent it

 I was hacked

I was loving this guy. Clearly not getting anywhere with any of his attempted scams, he turned it back round to tell me he had been scammed, within the last 30 seconds, and then had miraculously gained control of his account once again. I was genuinely impressed with his work ethic.

Despite going through a number of scams, it seemed 'Anna' still wasn't ready to give up – but I think deep down, he knew the game was up. He knew I knew he was a scammer. I knew that he knew that I knew he was a scammer. However, I respected him for trying all his scam efforts on me and I had to be honest with him.

I love a scammer

 Then marrier me

Well, that escalated quickly! I explained that I couldn't marry 'Anna' despite him being single and loving me and wanting to 'marrier' me. I told him that sadly he wasn't my type.

I only marry black Nigerian men

It was shame that the relationship would not work, because I would only marry Nigerian men. We both knew that this relationship couldn't continue. Or could it...

I'm one

Say, whaaaaat? I explained, it simply could not be true. I mean, the profile photo was that of a white man. The name? That was the name of a white woman. This simply could not be true.

 I love 🖤 you that's why I wanted to be sure you're real

'Anna' explained that he was indeed a Nigerian man and he lived in Lagos. He explained that his real name was Susseful. I asked him why he had lied to me, why he was lying to his followers by having a fake profile.

 I love 🖤 you that's why I wanted to be sure you're real

When I replied to Susseful to tell him that his response doesn't make any sense, his response was once again that he loved me. When I thanked him for being honest and advised that our conversation must now stop, Susseful advised that he needed help. He said he had no parents, he doesn't have a job, he doesn't have any money and he needed help.

It's at this point where you start questioning yourself. Was Susseful telling the truth? Was his name really Susseful? Who is really the bad guy here? If Susseful is real and telling the truth, then surely, I am the bad guy for just wasting his time and not giving him what he wants. Yeah, I'm stopping him from scamming other people – but am I also stopping someone from eating that day? Am I stopping someone from going hungry?

It was starting to have a bit of an effect on me. Was I doing more wrong than right here? Am I causing more harm by stopping people scam people for such small amounts of money? If people do get scammed for $20, is it really the end of the world? Does that money mean that people living in poverty get to eat? The question I suppose is if that $20 turns into regular, bigger amounts. After many months of interacting with scammers like this, I think my allegiance was shifting. It was difficult to not feel sorry for people who live in such an impoverished country and are doing what they can to feed themselves and their family.

Regardless, Susseful blocked me, so we never had the opportunity to 'marrier' each other.

I did think about stopping the conversations with scammers. I was spending a lot of time on my phone, and for what purpose? After all, I was a guy with a fake Instagram profile as well. Although I wasn't scamming people for money, I was still interacting with people who genuinely needed money with no intention of giving them any.

So, that's what I did. I stopped.

I stopped for a bit.

Just a few days.

When I next logged into Instagram, I probably had 60 messages. All from scammers. All with the intention of getting money from me. All from very very poor people.

I don't know why but one of the accounts stood out. It was an account not dissimilar to all the others. The profile picture looked a bit like Greg Davies. I thought I would message fake Greg Davies. So, I did.

I'm glad I did. The following is a conversation with 'William Graham'.

**BEHIND THE MAGICIAN'S CLOTH**

### William Graham
williamgramah108 · Instagram
60 followers · 0 posts
You follow each other on Instagram

View Profile

You see, he does look a bit like the host of Taskmaster. 'William' messaged back when I replied to his original message. It seemed like the normal kind of messages I would always get. However, I certainly didn't realise where this conversation would go.

William and I were getting to know each other, and I have to say there was a bit of a connection. William started with the love and romance scam by asking if I was single, what I did for living and if I had children. He was hoping that I would fall in love with him It didn't end like that. But I would like to think it ended up with an even happier ending.

After the usual back and forth, I found out that William's partner had died, and he was searching for a soul mate to spend the rest of his life with.

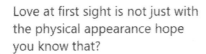

Love at first sight is not just with the physical appearance hope you know that?

You are so right William – 'Love at first Instagram message' really does have a nice ring to it. Someone, please get me the number of Clinton's Head Office. As time wore on, William was ever so more forward with his feelings towards me.

> I wanna let you know that
> something has being ringing in
> my heart since first time after i
> finish chatting with you, i have
> not meet you but i feel for you

After declaring his love for me and telling me he wanted to spend the rest of his life with me – it wasn't long before his messaging changed, and to continue with our conversation, he needed an iTunes card to 'update his system'.

> Please dear can you get me an
> iTunes card please

> I want to update my system

William wanted a $100 iTunes voucher to 'update his system'. How lucky we are in the western world, that Apple et al gives us these updates for free!

After a few more conversations where I started being a bit silly, and he kept steering the conversation back to him getting an iTunes voucher, I confronted 'William' and told him that obviously I knew that this was a scam, and I would appreciate an honest conversation with me. Incredibly, 'William' decided to tell the truth.

> Ok

> I am a scammer

> I know that you we block me

> And you we not chat me
> anymore

Usually at this point after I had confronted a scammer, they would block me and move on – but not 'William'. This was the first person I had spoken to that admitted they were a scammer, and the conversation continued.

I wanted to know more about scammers – what kind of cons and tricks they use, why they do it, if these cons are ever successful and if they have remorse if conning innocent people out of their money. 'William' advised he would speak to me, on one condition. Yeah, you guessed it... 'William' would talk to me if I got him an iTunes voucher. Was this in itself a con?

Maybe I was starting to feel bad after conversations with all these people over the last couple of years. All the people I had spoken to were real people. Real people hiding behind a fake profile. But all of them desperate for money. So, that's what I did. I went to Tesco and got a £50 iTunes voucher (hello, 2008 called!) and scratched off the film to reveal the numbers. I sent a photo of the numbers and receipt to 'William', and I waited to see if he would continue a conversation with me like promised, or if I would be blocked and he would move on to his next victim.

When I sent through the details, I kept refreshing his profile. Just waiting for the profile to change to show that he had blocked me. I must have refreshed about 50 times. But his profile was still there.

To my astonishment, 'William' replied and we kept talking to each other. He told me his name was Miracle, and he was a 20-year-old Nigerian living in Benin City. Benin City is the capital and largest city of Edo State and the fourth-largest city in Nigeria.

Miracle told me he goes to school most days; he goes to church every Sunday and prays for a better life for himself and his family. This is Miracle.

I had a few questions for Miracle to find out a bit more about some of the scams that happen across Instagram. The first question was why he does it. Unsurprisingly, the reason was money.

I want to feed my family

We don't have money here

I told Miracle that my name wasn't Pippa Pegg. I told him my name was James and I lived in the UK. At the time I had a few of these silly scenarios written down and had planned on putting a book together on it. I told Miracle about this I and asked if I could interview him for the book. Miracle agreed to this. Miracle told me that Nigeria is (unsurprisingly) a very poor country.

He said the government is corrupt and there are very little opportunities for jobs where he lives. He said that in Nigeria, the rich get richer, and the poor get poorer.

According to a recent report, 133 million Nigerians lack more than one essential survival need (good health, good living standards, primary education, and gainful employment). That makes up over 60% of the entire population. It's estimated that around 100 million Nigerians live below the poverty line. According to this report:

- 50% of Nigerians don't have access to clean energy for cooking.
- 47% of Nigerian don't have clean sanitation facilities.
- 29% of Nigerians don't have access to clean water.
- 26% of Nigerian children don't have the ability to go to school.

Unbelievably, some Nigerians use charcoal and even animal faeces to cook their food. Access to good cooking fuels, clean and single-use sanitation facilities, proximity to healthcare facilities, adequate food, and basic housing materials for shelter are the top needs Nigerians lack.

With these incredible statistics on show, it's no wonder that people will do whatever they can to survive. In the west, we live in such a privileged position where running water, education, our health system – in many ways, is all taken for granted. But, for millions of people across the world – these things are considered absolute luxuries.

After speaking with Miracle, it became very obvious that he was doing what he was doing to survive. He told me that apart from going to school, he made a little money cutting people's bushes, but it wasn't enough money to provide for him and his family. I asked him what kind of scams he takes part in – and he says he targets single women to attempt the 'love and romance' scam. He said it's very rare that he gets any success in this scenario and most people recognise it's a scam and block him.

Miracle said that it's easier to build relationships with lonely single western women and searches for these women across Instagram.

Although Nigeria is a massively poor country, in poor areas, luxury items are seen as great wealth. Nigerians (predominantly young men) are wanting to be seen having the latest iPhone, as much as a status thing more than anything. Despite all this horrifying statistics, a whopping 84% of Nigerians have mobile phones (UK is currently 95%). A mobile phone also means access to a whole world of opportunities too. It gives you the opportunity to interact with people all over the world, and the opportunity to try to earn money in whatever way that might be. Instagram gives scammers the platform to speak to anyone across the world, and if they can convince someone that they are someone else, there's an opportunity to extract money from them.

Only 50% of Nigerians have a bank account, meaning that the best way to get money from strangers is to obtain an iTunes voucher or Steam card, where they can quickly sell the credit on the street for money.

Miracle told me about the currency of the Instagram account itself. For scammers, your Instagram account is hugely valuable. If the account looks legitimate, if it has lots of followers and has been active for a while – then it could be sold. Here are some screenshots of conversations from WhatsApp that Miracle sent to me of scammers selling Instagram accounts.

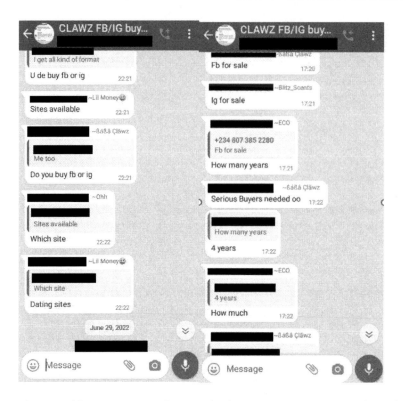

It's normal for scammers to have multiple Instagram accounts and use them as backup accounts. It means if their account does get taken down by Instagram, they can use their backup account(s) and carry on as before. Miracle showed me several of his Instagram accounts he has – some of them were legitimate businesses that had been hacked and the original owner could no longer gain access to.

Earlier, I talked about the 'online ambassador' con. In this instance, scammers will gain access to your account and there's very little you can do about it. Unless you can prove that the account has been hacked, the account will continue in the hands of the scammer. By this time of course, they have changed password/security back-up.

I was contacted by a scammer using the account 'Society of Women Writers WA'. Looking into the account, it looks legitimate – their bio states they are a *'Perth based writing organisation offering support, encouragement and information to women writers throughout Western Australia'*.

The scammer hadn't changed anything about the account at all, hadn't posted, but the account looked genuine (as it was genuine before it got hacked). It just means when you are getting messages from this account, you are more likely to believe them, as the account looks so trustworthy.

I contacted the Society of Women Writers WA to ask about their ordeal. They emailed back to say their account was hacked but declined to give an interview with me.

Back to the 'Society of Women Writers WA' account though. After conversations with the account about how to vote for them in an online ambassador program, I advised that I obviously knew they were a scammer, and that particular scam is awful and would never work on people. How little I knew...

Replied to you

1. Your scam is dreadful. That will never work.

It's works

I have use it hack so many people 😅

Here we go again. Another scammer who was willing to talk. His name was William, and he also lived in Benin City, Nigeria. William said he had hacked the account and was going to use it to post content on Bitcoin to get people to invest in the 'Bitcoin scam'. He said there was more money in using the Bitcoin investment scam and can get up to $500 with this ruse.

By posting Bitcoin content on the Society of Women Writers WA account, it gives it more legitimacy amongst their followers. It means that they can message the accounts followers, trying to get them involved in another scam. The good news for the scammer is that the account is already known to the victim, and trust has already been formed.

Back to William. He advised that it's the only way he can make money in Nigeria. He said there are no jobs for him, and he's not educated in a way where he has an opportunity to get a job. He scams people on Instagram to help feed himself and his parents. He talked about how important family was to him, his parents in particular, and wanted to help them for raising him. William explained that all his male friends use Instagram to scam people. He said that him and his friends use the 'bitcoin', 'online ambassador' and 'love and romance' scam.

After a bit more chatting, William was very surprised that I knew about these scams. I tried to impress him by using some of the Yoruba (Nigerian language) words I had learnt in the last couple of years. As stated earlier, the word 'Alaye' is used amongst online scammers to identify each other. It's the most common word used in all conversations on Instagram.

What does alaye stand for? ⌃

aláyé (colloquial, slang) **powerful or impactful person**. (colloquial, slang) thug. (Internet, text messaging, criminal slang) a code word used by scammers to reveal themselves to each other.

[w] https://en.m.wiktionary.org › wiki

alaye - Wiktionary

So, I was trying to impress William with some of my Yoruba language knowing skills. It turns out people from Benin City speak French as their main language, so I looked like a mad man[123].
Anyway, William explained that the 'dating scam' is more of a long-term con.

You have to date client online for a month plus before asking for money

Fans of mid 2000's BBC program Hustle will know all about the long con[124]. It was at this point that I asked William if he was OK telling me all this information about the murky world of scamming. I told him about the book I was writing and wonderfully, he agreed to talk about his life and experiences.

This is where there's a bit more going on. The Bitcoin scam goes through to an actual website, a real working website set up by scammers to look as legitimate as possible. William explained that the cost of setting up the website can be as much as $1,000 – so it looks as real – to get people to 'invest' their money. William said this way of life doesn't bring in a regular income and is pure luck depending on who is he speaking to. He says that western people can be gullible (although he didn't use that exact word) and he has some success, but

---

[123] Werey man.
[124] God, I loved Hustle. Go check it on iPlayer.

most people just block him. He said the bitcoin scam was quite popular at the moment – it seems people still don't believe the adage 'it's too good to be true.' When it comes to money, western people want more – well, everyone wants more. If there's an opportunity to get more money, people are interested.

We then had a bit of a chat about the football World Cup and said goodbye. The next couple of days, William and I talked less about scamming and just more about other things. At the time, the men's football World Cup was on, so we were talking about some of the games we had watched and made our predictions as to who would win the competition.

Two days later, William contacted me again.

That's right. William had sold his account to another person, and they were using the account to contact their followers attempting the 'ambassador scam'. I was sad that I wouldn't hear back from William again.

Back to my other friend from Benin City, Miracle. We would chat most days. We would talk about football. He was a Manchester United fan, and his favourite player was Cristiano Ronaldo. I nearly stopped speaking to him after this revelation. He asked me what I knew about Nigeria, and he taught me some of the foods that Nigerians eat. He taught me about a dish called garri[125], and I had quite the time explaining to him what marmite is.

Miracle asked if there was any opportunity for me to come and visit him. He couldn't understand why that wasn't a possibility. Perhaps being naïve, but he thought that everyone living in the west are rich and can do anything they want at all times. I explained to Miracle about the price of houses, food and general life.

At one point he messaged me and asked me what I was doing with my day. When I replied and said that I was going on a long bike ride, as I was in training for a charity bike ride – he had a very sweet reply.

> I went on a big bicycle ride today. I'm doing a charity bicycle ride soon trying to raise money for a cancer charity soon

Good luck James

I pray you should win

What a legend.

It was at this point where I spoke to a number of Nigerian scammers who all seemed quite open to having conversations with me. Daniel from Lagos explained that he was doing this simply for money, to help pay for his schooling. He admitted that he didn't like what he did, but he was doing this to try to make a better living for himself and his family. I spoke to another guy called Shedrack. After just a few messages with him, he explained as well why he was messaging me and what he does.

---

[125] An ingredient used to make the Nigerian food, Eba.

But the problem I don't have
work I don't go to school again
because of school fees

But I will love to go to so if I
have money that is why I started
scammed am so sorry for that

We had a conversation about a few things. Obviously, he wanted money from me, but I realised quickly I couldn't give money to everyone I was speaking to. But again, I thought to myself that $50 to me is very different to $50 to Shedrack. So, I went down to Tesco[126] again and got him an iTunes voucher.

He was very grateful, and we talked about our favourite foods. Shedrack's favourite food was pizza and egusi soup. After having difficulty previously explaining what marmite was to Miracle, I thought it best I didn't try the same mistake with Shedrack. Instead, I explained what my favourite food was. That was another error[127].

I also spoke to another scammer on Google Chat who wanted me to call him Tony. Tony was Nigerian and lived in Anambra State.

Tony said that there wasn't anything good about living in Nigeria. He had good friends, but there was nothing else to get excited about. Tony was a student and said he was studying Geophysics. He said he didn't know what the point of studying for this qualification was as there's no jobs available for people regardless of gaining qualifications.

---

[126] At least I was getting Clubcard points.
[127] Toad in the hole.

**Martinez Fab** Sat 19:55

Aight look, the thing with school here is
we all made a mistake starting it
The education system is corrupt
We don't know what we're learning
No good lectures always, they're always
looking for a way to extort from students
I mean we're tired but we have no other
option than to just finish what we started

Tony seemed more than happy to chat with me. Maybe he just felt he the opportunity to just rant at me about his circumstances. However, it was the first time that a scammer hadn't asked me for money. At no point in any of our conversations did he ask for anything.

**Martinez Fab** Sat 19:56

It's cool. I don't want you to feel sorry for
me I'm just being truthful

I asked Tony more about some of the scams he took part in. He said the most he ever scammed out of someone was $6,000. He said that was a love and romance scam. Tony said that in the love and romance scam, people give money over and over again. They truly believe, or really want to believe that they have found love. I'm sure they don't want to believe the truth. In my research for this book, I've read of people who have lost nearly £100,000 on this type of scam. All their savings gone because they (wanted) to believe they had found love.

I asked Tony if he felt bad scamming innocent people of their money. He said he did. Tony said if his circumstances were different, he wouldn't do this. He said he has no choice, and he does what he can do to survive. Tony said he stopped scamming for six months, but in the end, he had to go back to it to help provide for himself and his family. He said he had a 'fucked left lung' which needs daily medication which also costs money. He said he is hoping to get an operation to get it removed but doesn't know if that will ever happen.

**Martinez Fab** Mon 14:30

It's been there since childhood
Nothing new
Now, you see why we scam
We have no choice
If my country was like yours
Do you think I would?
NEVER
If I was in your country do you think I'd be
scamming? NO

Tony said he also operates the Bitcoin scam too. He said there's a website where people invest their money. It looks like a real Bitcoin site and people can see their investment go up. However, obviously it's all fake and they lose all their money.

Tony told me he has over 30 Instagram accounts. All 30 account are used to try and scam innocent people. He did say that Instagram have closed down some of his accounts, and he has lost money as he's been halfway through a con with someone when Instagram have closed the account.

Instead of setting up new accounts, Tony said he used to buy Instagram accounts from the dark web, but now has a vendor where he gets them. As discussed, the older an account, the more legitimate it looks. The more legitimate an account looks, the bigger chance that people will think it's legitimate.

After speaking to Miracle, Tony, Shedrack and William, you can understand why these people do what they do. Having a mobile phone gives them access to a whole new world, and with this, it gives them the opportunity to try and raise funds in a completely new, but ultimately, dishonest way.
By now, I think I was caught in the middle of these two worlds. Having heard from these people, you can hear the desperation in the words as they talk about what they will do to feed themselves and their family for the day. The next day brings the same challenges.

What would you do if you were in this situation?

## THE BIGGER PICTURE

What you have read so far has hopefully been some light-hearted silly conversations with Nigerian scammers to waste their time and data. After speaking to Miracle and others, you could see the plight that these were all in. But let's look at the bigger picture. In 2023 Briton's will lose an estimated £250m to scams across Meta's platforms of Instagram, Facebook and WhatsApp.

As a result, Meta is facing growing pressure from MPs in the UK, consumer groups and the UK banking sector over its failure to prevent the fraud on Facebook, Instagram and WhatsApp, where people are losing life-changing sums every day.

A recent investigation from The Guardian has revealed some of the human stories behind scams.

One Facebook user told The Guardian she was defrauded of her life savings and got pulled into debt, losing a total of £70,000, after being duped by an investment scam.

Scams across Meta are not just happening on Instagram. A recent scam on WhatsApp has scammers texting the words 'Hi mum' where fraudsters impersonate family members to get them to send large sums of money. Valerie, 73, a resident of the UK, handed over £2,000 to someone pretending to be her son, a small business owner who had borrowed money in the past. She said she would "never get over" the humiliation of being caught out this way.

TSB bank says there were huge fraud spikes originating from Meta-owned sites and apps in 2022, which were responsible for 80% of the cases it dealt with.

Many victims told The Guardian they had found it hard to report scams to Meta or that when they did, they received an automated response – or no reply at all. Lucy Powell, Shadow Digital, Culture, Media and Sport Secretary says, "Despite the eye-watering scale of scams online, the government had to be dragged into including fraud and scams in the shadow digital, culture, media and sport secretary online safety bill, only to delay and water it down at the last minute," she said.

"It's time for them to stop bowing to vested interests and stand up for consumers and victims."

The online safety bill (more on this later) currently going through parliament will require tech and social media platforms to remove scam adverts, while the government's new anti-fraud measures include asking tech firms to make it easier to report fraud and permitting banks to delay suspicious payments.

Robin Bulloch, the TSB chief executive, said he was deeply concerned by the high levels of fraud on Meta's sites. He said: "As the only UK bank with a fraud refund guarantee, we have unrivalled insight on this issue, and it is tragic to see UK households lose life-changing sums every day due to insufficient protection on Meta platforms."

Another banking bod, Matt Hammerstein, the chief executive of Barclays UK, echoed the situation saying, "It is in the interest of everyone that tech companies now join this fight in earnest, to prevent the unchecked growth of what is now the most common crime in the UK, costing the economy billions each year," he said. "If they are unwilling to act quickly enough on a voluntary basis, tech companies may need a financial incentive to act, so should then be required to contribute towards the reimbursement of victims based on a 'polluter pays' principle."

Starling Bank described Facebook as the "single biggest enabler of fraud" suffered by its customers, followed by Instagram. It withdrew all paid ads from Meta platforms in December 2021 in protest at its failure to tackle this problem.

"Government measures do not go far enough, and we are disappointed that the responsibility of reimbursing customers falls only on banks, while the social media platforms, where the fraud originated, are let off the hook" Starling Bank said in a statement. "These platforms, including Meta, profit from crime and yet remain beyond the reach of law."

When asked about scams on their platforms, Meta said fraud was an industry-wide issue, with scammers using increasingly sophisticated methods. "We don't want anyone to fall victim which is why our platforms have systems to block scams, financial services advertisers now have to be authorised and we run consumer awareness campaigns on how to spot fraudulent behaviour," Meta said in a statement.

## HOW TO AVOID SCAMS ON INSTAGRAM

Let's take a break from Meta and talk about some of the things you can do to help yourself from falling victim to a scammer on Instagram.

**Make your account private.**

Did you know your Instagram account is automatically set to 'public' by default, allowing anyone to see your posts. To protect your privacy, set your account status to 'private'. Then, only followers you approve can see your posts, make comments, find your posts via search, and send you direct messages. This is the easiest way that scammers won't be able to get you.

**Use a strong password.**

There are a few rules regarding passwords that apply to all your online accounts:

- Never use the same password on more than one account.
- Always use a complex password rather than something easy to figure out. Fun fact: The password '123456' appears in more than 23 million passwords across the world.
- Don't store your password list in an easily discoverable place.

Despite this sage advice, in 1996 I remember my dad writing his PIN on the back of his debit card as in his words "That's the best way for me to remember it". You can't argue with logic Dad. But you did have to argue with Santander when your debit card got stolen.

**Enable two-factor authentication.**

One of the best ways to protect your Instagram account from unwanted access is to enable two-factor authentication. When this security feature is turned on, it will take more than just knowing your login credentials to gain access to your account. When someone tries to log in from an unrecognised device, they will need to provide a unique authentication code. This code is sent via an authenticator app on your smartphone. This will straight away stop you falling prey to the 'ambassador scam'. Get on this, folks!

**Never click on suspicious links**

If you receive an unsolicited email purporting to be from Instagram, make sure it is legitimate before you do anything else to avoid falling for a scammer's strategies.

**Only buy from verified profiles**

Before you buy anything on Instagram, check to make sure the account you're dealing with is verified. All legitimate brands on Instagram will take the time to complete this step. You can easily do this by looking for the blue circle with a checkmark next to the account name. Despite writing this book and spending the last three years conversing with many scammers, I still got scammed by a ridiculous offer and sent money to an unverified Instagram seller[128]. Big thanks though Monzo, I got my money back pretty quickly.

**Keep track of third-party apps**

Over time, you have likely connected a number of third-party applications to your Instagram account. You should regularly review these applications to ensure no suspicious connections have been made. On your account you can see a list of all active, expired, and removed third-party applications here. Delete any you do not recognise or no longer use.

**Don't respond to unsolicited direct messages.**

If your Instagram account is set to public, anyone can direct message (DM) you. This is an open invitation for scammers to easily reach you. Don't do a what is known in the industry as a 'James Billington' and start replying to all the direct messages you get. Once you interact with one, you'll soon be down a rabbit hole where it's taking over your life. If you don't want to make your account private, then be vigilant when engaging with unsolicited DMs from people you do not know or recognise. If you suspect a DM to be a scam, report the account to Instagram and block the account. If you get a message from Keanu Reeves though, ask him what a casserole is.

**If it sounds too good to be true, it probably is.**

There's a reason this saying has been around forever. It usually (always?!) rings true. If you receive an incredible offer from somebody you don't know, chances are it's a scammer trying to scam you.

**Red flags**
Remember, pictures of red flags are broadly fine.

---

[128] 10 wrestling t-shirts for £25! Wazzzzzzup!

## REPORTING ACCOUNT TO INSTAGRAM

Hey, James – why don't you just ignore these messages, block the account and move on? It's a fair question, well made. Hey, James – why don't you just report the account and get Instagram to deal with it? It's another fair question, well made. Hey James, why don't you accept that you'll never buy another buy a pair of bootcut jeans from Burtons? Yes, can we stop with the fair questions please?!

As we have discussed the kinds of scams that occur across Instagram, and we've spoken to some of the people themselves that do this – let's now take a look at Instagram themselves and what they are doing to protect their users on their platform?

Meta are one of the biggest companies in the world, earning a reported $671 billion in 2021. To put that into context, that's earning $100 a year from every single person on the planet. Every single person on the planet. Even Hulk Hogan. Due to their size, you'd imagine they must have some pretty strict policies in place when it comes to reporting inappropriate content on their platform.

Instagram says it works to keep their platform *'appropriate, safe, and comfortable for all its users'*. With over one billion active users, it has its work cut out to keep up with all the reported content. So, let's take a look at this, shall we.

The good news is that it's very easy to report or block an account on Instagram. It's a very hard to miss, big red button. On its site, Instagram goes into details on the reasons why you can report content.

According to Instagram, you can report the following:

**A specific post:**
You can report a particular post because it's spam, it contains nudity or sexual activity, has hate speech or symbols, a post bullies or harasses, it contains false information, is a scam or fraud, promotes violence or dangerous organisations, encourages suicide or self-injury, promotes eating disorder or violates an intellectual property.

**The Instagram account:**
If you are reporting an Instagram account, it can be for a cornucopia[129] of

---

[129] Someone got a thesaurus for Christmas.

reasons.

- They are pretending to be someone else: Whether that's you, a celebrity or public figure, or business and organisation. Even Hulk Hogan.
- They are under 13 or pretending to be under 13 years old. Instagram requires everyone to be at least 13 years old before they can create an account. However, in some jurisdictions, the age limit needs to be higher.
- You can also report someone's Instagram account for a number of reasons such as spam, the sale of illegal or regulated goods, nudity or sexual activity, hate speech, bullying, harassment, scams and frauds or giving false information.

However, when you report an account or post, you won't always an update on the result of the complaint. It's often unclear what actually happens when you report an account on Instagram.

Once you report a post, account, or comment on Instagram, the company will get the notification and look at your complaint. Instagram states it will look at your report on a priority depending on if several others also report the same. You can ask your followers to report a problematic account or post. Yes, Instagram is telling its users to do more work to help sort the problem. Global Security Advisor, Jake Moore, says that the prevalence of scam accounts was 'probably the biggest unresolved issue with Instagram now'.

He stated 'When you report an account, it may not be viewed by an actual member of staff for a long period of time so to speed this up, you will need to get multiple people reporting the same account quickly after noticing the fraud. This pushes the account higher up the list to be looked at by a human.' Once Instagram validates your report, it will take appropriate measures to limit account/post reach. Instagram states they may ban or deactivate the reported account or post.

**What Instagram are doing about to try to stop scams occurring on their platform?**

This is content from the Instagram website: *Scams on Instagram happen when people create fake accounts or hack into existing Instagram accounts that you've followed. The scammers use these fake or compromised accounts to trick you into giving them money or personal information.*

*Things to watch out for:*

- *People who you don't know in person asking you for money.*

- *People asking you to send them money or gift cards to receive a loan, prize or other winnings.*
- *Anyone asking you to pay a fee in order to apply for a job.*
- *Accounts representing large companies, organisations or public figures that are not verified.*
- *People claiming to be from Instagram security asking you to provide account information (such as your username or password) or offering you account verification services.*
- *People asking you to move your conversation off Instagram to a less public or less secure setting, such as a separate email address.*
- *People claiming to have a friend or relative in an emergency.*
- *People who misrepresent where they are located.*
- *Messages that appear to come from a friend or a company you know that ask you to click on a suspicious link.*
- *Accounts that have a brief history on Instagram.*
- *Messages or posts with poor spelling and grammatical mistakes.*
- *People or accounts asking you to claim a prize.*
- *People or accounts that offer items at an extreme discount.*
- *Hulk Hogan doing Hulk Hogan things.*

They even go into details on their 'Staying Safe' section.

### Types of scams

**Romance scams:** *Romance scammers typically send romantic messages to people they don't know, often pretending to be divorced, widowed or in distress. They'll engage in online relationships claiming to need money for flights or visas. Their goal is to gain your trust, so the conversations may continue for weeks before they ask for money. Be vigilant of engaging in such conversations with people you don't know in real life.*

**Lottery scams:** *Lottery scams are often carried out from accounts impersonating someone you know or an organisation (such as a government agency or a social media platform). The messages will claim that you're amongst the winners of a lottery and that you can receive your money for a small advance fee. The scammer may ask you to provide personal information, such as your physical address or bank details which they can use for other criminal activities.*

**Loan scams**: *Loan scammers send messages or leave comments on posts offering instant loans, at a low interest rate for a small advance fee. Once an initial payment has been made, they may ask for more money to provide a larger loan or simply end the conversation and disappear with the payment. Avoid making any transactions to people that you don't know.*

**False investment scams:** *Scammers may promise unrealistic monetary benefits such as offering to convert a small amount of money into a larger sum (e.g., $100 = $1000) and solicit money from you. This false promise of return-on-investment results in the scammer disappearing with the payment. Some types of false investment scams to watch out for include "cash flipping" scams, Ponzi schemes or "get rich quick" schemes.*

**Job scams:** *Job scammers use misleading or fake job postings to try and get your personal information or money. Avoid job postings that sound too good to be true or that ask you to pay anything upfront. When clicking on a link from a job posting, watch out for websites that seem unrelated to the original job posting or that ask for sensitive information (e.g., government ID) but don't use secure (https) browsing.*

**Credit card fraud:** *Scammers use stolen financial information to make purchases online or to lure others into buying goods or services at a significantly lower price than the market price. If you notice suspicious activity on your credit card, you should report it to your financial institution or local law enforcement.*

**Paid subscription services:** *Scammers will offer the sale of paid subscription services or lifetime access to these paid subscription services for a one-off payment. Avoid purchasing subscription-based services from unknown third parties as scammers won't deliver the product or the product won't work as they claim it will.*

**Phishing scam[130]:** *Phishing is when someone tries to get access to your Instagram account by sending you a suspicious message or link that asks for your personal information. If they get into your account, a scammer may have access to things such as your phone number or email address. They may also change your password to lock you out of your account.*

**Inauthentic sellers:** *Inauthentic or misleading sellers may try to use under-priced items to lure buyers into a scam. They may try to create a sense of urgency to get buyers to act quickly, request payment through a non-secure method or misrepresent their location in their posts.*

This is good work Instagram! At least you are telling people of some of the ways that people can be scammed. It might be hidden away on your website, but at least it's there.

Instagram tell us what to look out for, how to report it and what to report. So, surely that's nice and easy, right?! Surely once an account gets reported, it will

---

[130] Usually from someone called Rod. Am I right?

be investigated thoroughly, and if found to be violating any of Instagram's rules as shown above - it gets shut down automatically and the user can no longer set up another Instagram account, right? If you think it's that easy, I have some bitcoin to sell you...

If an account gets reported and Instagram decides they have broken their rules, they have the authority to close that account down. However, there's no reason why the user cannot simply set up a new account. All you need to create an Instagram account is an email address. It takes two minutes to create a Gmail[131] account. Once that email address has been created, there's no issue in the user creating a new Instagram account and chancing their arm again with whatever scam they want. This makes sense in the fact that many of the scam accounts that I dealt with have a 'new' icon next to them.

## WHAT HAPPENS WHEN YOU REPORT SOMEONE ON INSTAGRAM

Instagram reviews reports, but it isn't always clear how quickly they act. For every account that I have come across, I have reported it as either 'possible scam and fraud', 'nudity or sexual activity' or 'hate speech'. Over the last couple of years, that's hundreds, probably thousands of times I have reported scammers. During the process of writing this book, it does appear that Instagram has become more open and honest with its users on what has happened to accounts that its users report.

Previously, it was very hit and miss in terms of what the result of reporting an account would be. However, you now have access to your 'Support Requests' page on Instagram which shows you the status of your report.
That is the good news. Meta should obviously be open and honest with its users around reporting. Sadly, that is where the good news stops.

Over the last two years, I have dealt with thousands of accounts whose goal is simply to scam people and illegally gain funds from innocent people. Do Meta do enough to stop scam accounts? Well, you can be the judge of this with these replies to reports I made to Instagram regarding these two random accounts: One particular account that I reported was the user was sending me repeated unsolicited d[132] pics. This was the incident report I received from Instagram.

---

[131] or Hotmail, am I right Ceefax Generation?!
[132] Dick.

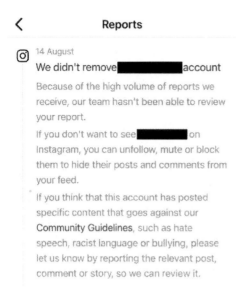

It's an incredible response isn't it from global billion-dollar corporation. A company with a revenue of six hundred and seventy-one billion dollars in a single year. Yes, we know you have been sent numerous unsolicited dick pics, but we as a business are too busy earning sweet coin to be dealing with your report! The good news is that you can block the account yourself. Let's not attempt at solving the problem, let's just click the 'block button' – because no doubt the person sending me a picture of his cock and balls will no doubt learnt his lesson. Will he though? Will he bollocks.

I was astounded at the lack of action Meta takes on reported content. Because of the high volume of reports that we receive, our team hasn't had time to be able to review this report. Oh, boohoo[133]! Everyone, please say a prayer for little old Instagram and their limited resources. Fear ye not though Instagram, as I have thought of a detailed plan of action to help with your Report Team, so they can deal with more reports. It's a simple model. It's a simple premise. Like all great ideas, this is not revolutionary or groundbreaking. It's the right idea at the right time – and it will so much help you at least with the backlog of complaints that your poor little company has to go through. Here we go...

**HIRE SOME MORE FUCKING PEOPLE, YOU COCKWOMBLES!**

I was so disturbed by the lack of action that Meta had taken on these reported accounts, I decided to delve a little deeper. As stated, through my time on this account, I have reported hundreds of accounts, and so I thought I would look at

---

[133] Not the online retailer targeting 18–30-year-olds.

the last 100 accounts I had reported and do some analysis on what has happened to these accounts since I reported them. I looked at my 'Support Requests' page and looked at reports from August/September 2023.

Those 100 reports were made up of the following violations:

- Hate speech – 22.
- Nudity or sexual activity – 19.
- Scam/fraud – 52.
- Miscellaneous – 7.

**HATE SPEECH**

Out of the 22 accounts I had reported for hate speech:

- Instagram took action on 41% of them, for not following their Community Guidelines. As a result of this, Instagram may give the account holder a warning, they may limit what they can do on Instagram or remove their account.
- 32% of the reports were closed because 'of the high volume of reports, we couldn't review this chat'.
- 27% of reports are still open, yet to be investigated by Instagram.

Going by this analysis, 59% of all accounts reported for hate speech are not resolved. With a mixture of automation and manual checking, it should be quite easy to identify what is classed as hate speech and what is not. For a company the size of Meta to unresolve 59% of reported hate speech across their platform is pretty shocking.

But it gets worse.

**NUDITY OR SEXUAL ACTIVITY**

Of the 100 reports I filed, 19 were nudity or sexual activity. In terms of Instagram's policy on nudity, it says *'We know that there are times when people might want to share nude images that are artistic or creative in nature, but for a variety of reasons, we don't allow nudity on Instagram. This includes photos, videos and some digitally-created content that show sexual intercourse, genitals and close-ups of fully-nude buttocks. It also includes some photos of female nipples, but photos in the context of breastfeeding, birth giving and after-birth moments, health-related situations (for example, post-mastectomy, breast cancer awareness or gender confirmation surgery) or an act of protest are allowed. Nudity in photos of paintings and sculptures is OK too.'* So, it rules

out sending unsolicited pictures of your spam javelin to someone.
From the 19 accounts I reported:

- 58% of those were closed because 'of the high volume of reports, we couldn't review this chat'.
- 32% were still open reports.
- 5% of accounts were removed for breaking their Community Guidelines.
- 5% of account were not removed as it was deemed to be inoffensive content.

In total, 95% of all reported content for nudity or sexual activity is not resolved. Like hate speech, automation and manual intervention should easily identify what is and isn't allowed across Instagram and the fact that 95% of users walk away without any punishment is something that needs addressing. Going by these statistics, you can send a picture of your dick to anyone, and there's just a 5% chance that Instagram will do anything about it.

If only 5% of accounts are being punished by Instagram, it means 95% of accounts are getting away with it, and no doubt continuing to send whatever content they want to whoever they want. Research by Professor Jessica Ringrose from 2020 concluded that 76 percent of girls aged 12-18 had been sent unsolicited nude images of boys or men.

As a result of these distressing figures, the UK Government brought in a new Online Safety Bill in March 2022 which aims at making social media firms more responsible for users' safety on their platforms.

The Online Safety Bill has taken years to agree and will force firms to remove illegal content and protect people from some legal but harmful material. Platforms such as Instagram will need to show they are committed to removing illegal content including:

- cyber-flashing
- child sexual abuse
- controlling or coercive behaviour
- extreme sexual violence
- illegal immigration and people smuggling
- promoting or facilitating suicide
- promoting self-harm
- animal cruelty
- selling illegal drugs or weapons
- terrorism
- the sharing of "deepfake" pornography.

As a result of the new bill, Technology secretary Michelle Donelan says, "The regulator will be working even more hand in hand with those social media platforms and you'll see them changing the way that they're operating", she added.

But the complexity of the act does cause her concerns that big tech companies will challenge parts of it in court.

Imran Ahmed of the Centre for Countering Digital Hate welcomed the passage of the bill saying, "too much tragedy has already befallen people in this country because of tech companies' moral failures".

But digital rights campaigners the Open Rights Group said the bill posed "a huge threat to freedom of expression with tech companies expected to decide what is and isn't legal, and then censor content before it's even been published".

Lawyer Graham Smith, author of a book on internet law, said the bill had well-meaning aims, but in the end, it contained much that was problematic.
He said it was "a deeply misconceived piece of legislation", and the threat it posed to legitimate speech was likely to be "exposed in the courts".

Popular messaging services such as Meta and Signal have threatened to refuse to comply with powers in the bill that could be used to force them to examine the contents of encrypted messages for child abuse material.

However following statements made the government about these powers in the Lords, Meredith Whittaker, the president of Signal, said that they were "more optimistic than we were when we began engaging with the UK government".

In terms of cyber-flashing, the change in law means that anyone who sends a photo or film of a person's genitals, for the purpose of their own sexual gratification or to cause the victim humiliation, alarm or distress may face up to two years in prison.

## SCAM/FRAUD

Of the 100 reports I looked at, 52 were classed as scam/fraud. Now, this is a bit more difficult to decipher whether accounts are attempting to scam or defraud you. The accounts I reported all follow the same criteria. They were are mainly new accounts, they all follow more people than have followers, they initiate direct messages and every single time they start private conversations with the goal being to extort money through a scam.

From the 52 accounts reported for scam/fraud:

- 83% of those were simply closed because 'of the high volume of reports, we couldn't review this chat'.
- 13% of the reports were still open.
- 2% of the accounts were removed for breaking their Community Guidelines.
- 2% were reviewed and the content was not removed.

Which means, a mind boggling 98% of all reported accounts for scam/fraud had no action taken on them, and those users are free to continue to try to extort money from other users on their platform. Just 2% of all accounts reported for scam/fraud had action on their account for not following Instagram's Community Guidelines.

Clearly this figure is hugely alarming for the users of Instagram. If someone reports an account for scam/fraud, and Instagram doesn't do anything because 'of the high volume of reports and that account scams another innocent body, where does the responsibility lie?

If 83% of all reported scams are not dealt with because you as a business can't deal with the amount of users reporting this, then surely you need to look at the bigger picture and try to make changes to help protect your users?
My reporting led me to more questions than answers. My next step was to speak to someone from Instagram to give them the report on my findings and ask what they are doing to make Instagram a 'safer place'. Being a multinational corporation, you'd expect lots of ways you can contact Instagram to speak to someone. Turns out, outside of the Help Centre, there is just one email address for you to contact Instagram. I was told that it was very rare that Instagram would reply to individuals. Regardless, I messaged and asked that it would be lovely if I could interview someone within Instagram to talk about the company's policies when it comes to fraud and scams, and what more they could to deal with the problem. The good news was I did actually get a reply.

The bad news was...

Hi,

You've reached us at a channel that we no longer support. Please visit the Help Center to find answers to many frequently asked questions and up-to-date forms you can use to contact us:

https://emea01.safelinks.protection.outlook.com/?url=http%3A%2F%2Fhelp.instagram.com%2F&data=05%7C01%7C%7C9109d97fb9254054cef708db6a7a259d%7C84df9e7fe9f640afb435aaaaaaaaaaaa%7C1%7C0%7C638220845066912175%7CUnknown%7CTWFpbGZsb3d8eyJWIjoiMC4wLjAwMDAiLCJQIjoiV2luMzIiLCJBTiI6Ik1haWwiLCJXVCI6Mn0%3D%7C3000%7C%7C%7C&sdata=HNDtn1xWhecroDSrOrPcxgB72Lv%2B2f113aJLVEQJjK4%3D&reserved=0

We apologize for the inconvenience.

Sincerely,
The Instagram Team

With the results of my analysis on reported content and the lack of visibility from Instagram, it seems Meta are doing as little as possible to help protect its users. As a huge multi-national corporation that 26% of the world's population over 13 years of age use, maybe Instagram believe they are above the law. It's down to governments and corporations to hold Meta to account to give the best possible experience to its users.

So, what can be done to make Instagram to protect its users?

**BETTER REPORTING**

Clearly if you are reporting an account for them sending a cavalcade of dick pics, you would hope that your report is looked into, investigated and if found guilty, then the account would be removed. You wouldn't expect to have a reply to the report to state they're too busy. Instagram need to completely overhaul their reporting system.

31 August

**Your report has been closed**

Because of the high volume of reports that
we receive, we couldn't review this chat. We
understand that this may be frustrating and
we're working on improving our review
process.

There's still more that you can do to control
your experience on Instagram. To stop
getting messages and calls from someone,
you can block their account. You can also
hide new message requests with offensive
words, phrases and emojis by turning on
"Hidden words" in your privacy settings.

1 Previous Message

*'We understand that this may be frustrating and we're working on improving
our our review process'*. Like everyone, I wait with bated breath as to what
improvements these will be and when they will be implemented.

## SECURITY CHECKS

Clearly, it is very easy to open up a new Instagram account. Too easy. During
my interaction with scammers in the £2m armed robbery fiasco, I created three
new Instagram profiles that probably took me five minutes in total. To be fair,
most of those five minutes was spent thinking up the names 'Little Tina' and
'Medium Dennis'. Clearly something needs to be done to make sure that when
accounts are set-up, they should have identification checks put in place. If users
had to register an account by uploading some form of identification, would this
deter scammers?

## AUTO MESSAGES

One of the recent improvements on X (formerly Twitter) has been to address
misinformation across their platform. In a world where anyone can say
anything to anybody with little or no consequences, X gives its users context on
tweets that give misinformation. For example, if someone sends a tweet
around Covid vaccines, there's an automatic content below that message to say
that it might be false and it provides a link to verified facts.

Instagram could work with something like this. If a scammer sends a message
to someone, chances are those two users only have a small amount of 'shared
followers'. If this is the case and a DM is sent from a scammer to a potential
victim, Instagram could auto send content at the bottom of the message to
warn them of the dangers of being scammed, and to be careful on who you are

messaging.

There's no doubt that Instagram can do more to protect its users away from scammers. The account I have has over 4,500 followers. Every single one of those are scammers. Every single one. Apart from the 12 Keanu Reeves accounts. They are all Keanu Reeves obviously.

Quite clearly, unless major governments look into Meta as a company and realise that more needs to be done, nothing will change. Instagram have made it as easy as possible to create an account for a reason. They know that having more users means more revenue and more advertisers, so whether to the accounts are legitimate is not their concern. Meta has bigger issues to look at. Since Facebook officially became Meta in October 2021, the company has lost more than two-thirds of its stock market value. Just over a month before the rebrand, Meta, hit an all-time stock market high. But, just a few weeks later, the revelations of whistleblower and former Facebook employee Frances Haugen proved damaging.

Haugen leaked thousands of internal company documents to The Wall Street Journal, revealing the extent to Meta had prioritised profit over dealing with hate, violence and misinformation on its platforms.

In 2022, The Irish Data Protection Commission (DPC) announced a penalty of €405m (£349m) against Instagram in relation to an alleged failure to protect children's data. Meta has been a particular target of the DPC; in the last year, the DPC has issued three fines against Facebook, WhatsApp and Instagram for violations of the General Data Protection Regulation (GDPR).

The DPC investigation into Instagram began nearly two years ago in September 2020 following concerns regarding how children's user data was being processed and protected by Instagram. The allegations are that:

- Children (users between 13 and 17 years old) using Instagram were allowed to activate 'business accounts'; however, given default privacy settings for business accounts, operating such accounts, resulted in the publication of child user's personal contact information (e.g. phone number and/or email address).
- As part of the Instagram user registration process, the platform had a setting through which child user accounts could, by default, be 'public'. In such instances, the individual (child) user would have to know to change the account settings to 'private'.

Just for the record, I'm on Team Irish Data Protection Commission.

In February 2022, Meta made stock market history by losing $237 billion in one single day, making it the biggest one-day valuation drop in U.S. history.
So, it does seem that Meta has problems already that it needs to address, but there's no doubt it needs to do more to help combat fraud on its platforms.

**IT'S TIME TO SAY GOODBYE**

Well, here we are coming towards the end of the book. Thanks so much for taking a chance on this book and kudos for making it this far.

Sadly though, there is no encore. This is not like where you go and see Shed Seven where you can clap, cheer, whoop and holla and they will play more songs. No matter how much you want, I won't be knocking on your door with a couple more chapters. It really is the end. I hope that you've had a little bit of fun. It's fair to say that there's been a few escapades with these scammers. On top of this, I have had more dick pics sent to me than I really should have[134]. I hope that the book has opened up your eyes on the often-murky world of Instagram. For the majority of people, Instagram is all about cat pictures and looking at people's happiest/non-reality moments, but there's certainly a lot more to the platform than meets the eye.

The account that I started this little adventure is still running, but I think it's best for my marriage that I stay logged out of it forever. If I had a son, I would give him the password to the account on my deathbed. Well actually, I'd probably send him a message on Instagram and ask if he could vote for me in an ambassador program. In fact, you, my dear reader, can have the password for the account. The account name is Pippa Pegg, and the password is 'WrestleMania35?!'. See if you can access it, and maybe sell it on the dark web.

For the last three years, I have pretty much been on Instagram for hours each day speaking to scammers. I dare not look at my 'activity log' on my iPhone[135] – it will make for pretty bleak reading.

The creator of Wordle got it right. Just do it for 5 minutes each day (and then sell it for an undisclosed seven figure sum). It's probably not great staying up until 1am some nights making up fake emails from greengrocers talking about offers on lemons. My careers advisor at school never said this would happen to me. Nor did Gypsy Lee, the fortune teller reading I had in 1996 at the Bullring market in Birmingham[136].

However, as much fun it has been to go on some odd adventures with scammers, it's important to know the reasoning why these people do it. The people I spoke to are from Nigeria and Ghana – both countries with huge poverty and very little hope for people growing up in these countries. These countries offer very little in terms of employment – so people have to find

---

[134] One
[135] Someone's earning.
[136] Might have been the same woman.

alternate ways to feed themselves.

With technology – a mobile phone allows them to contact people across the world and look to make money in whatever way they can to help survive. To them, obtaining $50 from a westerner means them providing food for their family. There's a stereotype from scammers that people in the western world are all rich. In many ways, we are. We may not be millionaires, but we have access to education, healthcare and Channel 5. We have running water; we have Fray Bentos pies, and we have a bed to sleep on each night.

When I spoke with Miracle and he opened up about being poor and providing food for his family, was I being meta-scammed!? Possibly – who knows? What I do know is, although $50 is a lot of money, I am in a very privileged position. I have a job that provides a regular and steady income. I have a roof over my head, I have access to all the things I need, including eight seasons of Quincy on DVD. $50 is a lot less money to me than it is to Miracle. There's absolutely no doubt that scammers are in an incredibly difficult position – a life of poverty, a life of not know where their next meal is coming from.

We should probably also address the word 'scammer'. Over the last couple of years, and having spoken to Miracle, Shedrack, William and Tony about their lives – I don't feel entirely comfortable using the term 'scammer'. I believe it's wrong we should be using that word that has such negative connotations. Yes, what they are doing is unethical – having fake profiles, lying and taking money from innocent people. However, in their shoes, we would probably all do the same. With no idea how they are going to survive the day/week/month, and being in such a perilous position, I do find it unethical to be using that term.

What is interesting, is that from the outside, we see these young men lying and cheating people out of money. But, Nigeria is a highly religious country. They all believe in God. They all believe that they are grateful for being on Earth, and that God will provide a way to lead them to a better life. I've had many conversations with Nigerians over the last couple of years on religion. Miracle couldn't believe that I didn't go to church every Sunday. In their world where poverty, disease and corruption is so prevalent, you would think that people wouldn't believe in God, questioning why God put them in this position. However, it's the cynical 'privileged' Western world that is becoming more and more atheist.

We're also in a place where we need to ask Instagram why more is not being done to stop this happening? I'd suggest we shouldn't be asking; we should be demanding. How can a company as big as Meta not investigate reported content simply because they are 'too busy'? If every time my wife asked me to put the bins out, and I replied 98% of the time that I was too busy, it wouldn't be long before I was put inside the bin myself. It staggers me that Meta seem to be getting out of not doing more to protect people. More needs to be done by Meta to help keep people safe on their platform. To Meta, the most important thing is having as many Instagram accounts as possible to help generate more advertisers to the site. By having little or no measures in place, anyone can create another and another Instagram profile. Governments should be pushing Instagram to be more accountable.

Instagram's advice on their website about scams is very pertinent. If something is too good to be true, it usually is. That applies in real life too. Unless you are my wife reading this – and in that case, you really have landed on your feet. I'll put the bins out when I have finished this chapter. My advice to anyone who receives messages that appear to be too good to be true – is to use that big red 'report' button.

It's also mind boggling that Instagram has such poor customer service options. There's no phone number to call for help, there's no email to send for help. There's no chat function. There is literally nothing. Just a help centre, which for all intents and purposes, should probably just be renamed 'centre'.
For me, it's been a really odd time putting this book together. It wasn't until I had a break from Instagram for a couple of months and then revisited it, did I realise how much content I had on this. The first thing I would do in the morning is check my Instagram and begin replying to scammer emails. Thankfully this book can give me some finality and I can close the account down for good and actually speaking to people in real life once again.

A couple of months before I'd finished the book, my mum died. One minute you are replying to scammers about lemons, and then something like this happens. It was a big shock, and amongst the sadness and anger, I am still trying to put all the pieces of that together. However, it did make me think about what I have been doing over the last three years with this. It has taken over my life in some ways. There's no doubt I could have spent more time with family and friends instead of being on this app. I have sent thousands of messages to scammers – and for what purpose? For putting together some silly scenarios? For highlighting the living conditions of people living in Nigeria? For pointing out the failures of a massive corporation such as Meta? I'm glad that I can have some closure on this. I can now pay more attention to my family, my friends, and focus a bit more on my wonderful wife.

So, as I log out of Instagram for the final time, I hope that I have opened your eyes about a number of the scams that people use on Instagram to get you to part you with your money. Hopefully you have learnt how to keep your Instagram safe and away from the hands of scammers. I hope that it's been a balanced look at the murky underbelly of Instagram. With 10% of all Instagram accounts being scammers or bots, there's an estimated 95 million accounts looking to take something from you. However, scammers are human beings. Human beings living in poverty. Human beings looking for a better life. Hopefully though you are now well versed in Instagram scams. However, you should know that scammers are always coming up with new initiatives, new ways of getting you to part with your hard-earned money.

For example, I heard about a new scam where people from Nigeria pretend to be a white man from England who writes a book about the murky world on Instagram, mentions the now defunct electric retail 'Tandy' a massive 47 times and get you to pay up to £15 for it. That would never work as a scam though, right?

Alaye.

**THANK YOU**

If you managed to get this far, thanks so much (and well done!). I do really appreciate you taking time to read the book. If you purchased it – thanks so much, you are officially a legend.

This is the first book I have ever written. I really wanted to for it to be more than just a silly book of timewasting Instagram messages. I wanted to give you, the reader, a look at the other side of things and hopefully make up your mind on Instagram scammers.

This is a self-published publication and as such, it's just me writing, promoting, and publishing. However, I am really proud of the book, and I would love as many people to get their eyes on it as possible.

If you have social media in the form of Instagram, Facebook, X, Vine etc, then I would really appreciate if you could share your thoughts on it. Word of mouth is the best form of promotion. You can also write a review on Amazon too. The more reviews that show on there, the better. That would be really amazing of you. Let me know your seven item English breakfast in the reviews too. That would certainly confuse the Amazon algorithm.

If you thought it was dogshit, keep your thoughts to yourself, though obvs.

Oh, and also.

I'm contesting for an ambassador spot at an online influencer program. Could you vote for me?

Thanks again for reading.

James

## ABOUT THE AUTHOR

James Billington is a former Mayor of Stafford[137], a former stand-up comedian[138], one half of the band Das Ingtons[139], a former contestant on Countdown[140] and a full-time bell-end.

He lives in Nottingham with his wife and cat, Bobo Brazil.

---

[137] Sort of.
[138] Failed.
[139] Legends.
[140] I did get an eight-letter word.

Printed in Great Britain
by Amazon

67a8be71-25ed-474a-b00b-6e9c857ce057R01